BReaKiNG iNTo HoLLyWooD

www.breakingintohollywood.org

ALSO BY ANGELA M. HUTCHINSON

Charm Kids

www.thecharmkids.com

BReaKiNG iNTo HoLLyWooD

ANGELA M. HUTCHINSON

CreateSpace
Scotts Valley, CA

Printed by CreateSpace, Scotts Valley, California
An Amazon.com Company.

To order additional copies of this book, visit www.bih-ent.com.

Book proceeds go to B.i.H. Entertainment, a for profit company.

Library of Congress Control Number: 2008909888

ISBN 978-1-4392-1591-3

Printed in the United States of America.

First Paperback Edition

10 9 8 7 6 5 4 3 2 1

"Breaking into Hollywood made me realize that there is a LOT more I can control in my career than I first thought. I realize the only person that can stop me, is ME."
Bryan Irzyk, *Actor* **– CSI**

"Breaking into Hollywood is a fantastic resource! It's an organization that provides essential career information, as well as an opportunity to meet mentors and friends pursuing a similar path."
Valerie Meraz, *Vice President,*
Content Acquisitions **– Showtime Networks**

"No matter what area of entertainment is in your dreams, let Breaking into Hollywood help you to make those dreams come true!"
Kathie Fong Yoneda, *Writer/Author* **–**
The Script-Selling Game

"Breaking into Hollywood is a phenomenal organization. It's a fantastic opportunity for any artist who is smart and serious about a career in Hollywood."
Wendi Niad, *Literary Manager* **–**
Niad Management

"I commend aspiring artists for taking the time to better themselves. I only wish I had such an organization [like BiH] to learn from when I was starting out."
Jennifer Basa, *Producer* **– The Amazing Race**

Above quotes are in reference to Breaking into Hollywood,
the 501(c)(3) non-profit organization based in Los Angeles.

CoNTeNTS

aCKNoWLeDGeMeNTS

To my *A-List* team —

My *amazing* husband Arthur,
amusing son Alexander, *adorable* daughter Alyssa,
altruistic mother Antoinette and *audacious* father Alvin;
admirable friends Sarah-Elizabeth, Mary Nicole and Maria;
awesome assistants Yvonne, Neha, Dominique and Alaric;
artistic BiH Board of Directors, Staff, Interns and Mentees;
accomplished mentors Angelia, Leeza, Valerie, Debbie,
Chemin, Tiffany and Pamela.

PReFaCe

Dear Reader,

Are you pursuing a dream that has made you weary and you need to be recharged? Do you have a dream you want to live out, but are scared of the unknown or afraid of failing? Or maybe you lack the money and resources needed to begin or to continue your pursuit?

If you are passionate about a dream, this memoir can energize you to achieve it. The dream-making process can indeed be challenging to endure. If you tenaciously pursue your goals until they are accomplished, neither self-defeat nor rejection will be able to hinder your success.

Let *BReaKiNG iNTo HoLLyWooD* empower you to bring your dream into fruition.

Seize the journey!

Angela M. Hutchinson

oNe

A Blockbuster Night

In a million years, I would have never imagined a person discovering their talent inside a video store—until it happened to me. Wearing a tank top and comfy shorts, I was browsing videos with my mother, trying to find a suitable movie for our cozy ladies' night at home. For nearly two hours, we read movie synopsis after synopsis. We are both very picky and not only had to agree on a movie, but also had to select one that neither of us had seen before. To this day, my husband calls Blockbuster "Angela's Disneyland" because I can easily spend an hour searching for a movie that fits my mood.

After pacing down the last aisle of videos, my mother approached me and said, "I didn't see anything worth renting. Did you?"

"Nada. The movie I really want to see is about a TV reporter so desperate for a promotion that she decides to produce an undercover story on her celebrity friends to expose their secret lifestyles," I said.

"Sounds juicy," she replied.

"One of the celebs, a basketball player, is an alcoholic. And his girlfriend, a model, struggles with anorexia and a drug addiction," I said in a TV trailer voice.

"Go on," my mother said, perking up.

"There's also a sitcom actor who is abusive to his wife, a professional dancer. She is having an affair with one of the basketball player's friends. The actor suspects his wife is cheating on him with her best male friend, a renowned photographer, who unexpectedly receives fatal news that changes the course of his life forever," I revealed.

"What finally happens to everyone?" my mother asked anxiously.

"We'd have to watch the movie to find out. But basically, while the TV reporter is producing the exposé, she is being backstabbed by her boss and eventually decides enough is enough. Unfortunately, it's too late—all of her celebrity friends have been thrown into a whirlwind of chaos," I conveyed.

"What's the name of it?" my mother asked.

I paused and stared blankly at the air.

"*Hollywood* ... no, *Hollywood Chaos*," I said with pride.

My mother started eyeing the row of videos where I was standing.

"Where is it? Let's get it!" she said.

I came out of my stare and looked at her, a bit confused.

"Huh?" I asked.

"We should definitely rent it!" she said while scanning the video shelf.

"Mother, you're kidding right?" I said with a smirk.

"No, it's perfect for tonight," she replied. "And neither of us have seen it."

"Mom, I was just saying that's the kind of movie I'm in the mood to see. It doesn't actually exist," I said.

"What do you mean?" she asked, arching her brow.

"I just made all of that up," I said.

"Right now?" she asked.

"Yeah. I thought about the type of movie I would like to see and was hoping I could find something like that in here," I explained.

"You created that right now, Angie, since we've been in the store?"

I nodded.

"Honey, you need to go write it," she said with such sincerity.

"Write it?" I asked cluelessly.

"You heard me," she replied.

"Mother, you are too funny," I chuckled. "I can't write a movie. I don't know how. I majored in engineering, remember?!"

"Which means you're a smart cookie. Go get a book on how to write a movie, and then write it," she instructed me.

"*Hollywood Chaos*?" I asked in a baffled voice.

"It's a Blockbuster," she declared.

The next morning, I eagerly drove to our local mall in Calumet City, Illinois. After a pit stop at the Cinnabon kiosk, I headed straight for the book store. A friendly saleswoman greeted me as I entered and asked how she could be of assistance. I inquired about a book on 'how to write a movie'. She guided me to a shelf of books on scriptwriting. I flipped through a couple. They seemed so theoretical and made me think it would be very difficult to learn how to write a movie. Suddenly, one caught my eye, "How to Write a Movie in 21 Days" by Viki King.

"This'll be a perfect summer project!" I thought to myself.

I purchased the book and gave myself 21 days to write my movie. First, I made an outline of my idea, did some research, and then wrote the script, all within just three weeks. I've heard it takes some writers a year to complete a script and sometimes even several months to crank out even a bad first draft. Many writers have a block for days, weeks, or even months. Not I, at that point in my pursuit. Freshly passionate about writing, I was determined not to allow any hindrance prevent me from accomplishing my goal.

With my first completed script in hand, I asked myself, "Now what? How am I going to get my script made into a movie if I live in Chicago?"

It was then I decided to move to Hollywood to get my movie onto the big screen. For those of you who are not in the entertainment field, that might seem like a realistic plan. But for those of us in Hollywood, we all know that although not impossible to achieve, it was indeed a goal that was easier said than done.

The passion I had for my dream was like that of a curious toddler with no established fears. The innocence of a child is a trait every entrepreneur should strive to obtain. It is that naive passion that allows one to pursue a dream—neither afraid to fail, nor fearful to try.

TWO

Ask Me About the Party Cruises

It was the beginning of the summer after graduating from college when I decided to work diligently at any decent job that could help me save money to move to L.A. First, I worked at a clothing boutique in the mall for a few weeks. I quickly discovered that wasn't for me because I kept seeing people from my high school. I felt embarrassed working in the mall with a college degree. So of course I moved on to the next best option: a waitress job at Hooters!

During my first day as a Hooter girl, I shadowed a waitress. Most of the men gave their order with their eyes glued to her chest. I then knew there was no way I could work there without being rude to the male customers. Not to mention how cheap the tips were for such beautiful and friendly women. Needless to say, my first day was my last.

The next job I tried was telemarketing. I was great at it and reached my daily goals. However, the problem was the amount of money I was making. It would take me until next summer to save enough cash to move out west. And I was ready to pursue my dream ASAP.

One night after a long day at work, I plopped onto my bed and lay on my back. I extended my feet against the pepto-bismol pink walls of the bedroom I had slept in as an infant. Yes, I was still living at home with an engineering degree from the University of Michigan. Sure, I could have blamed the school for coning me into accruing $100,000 of school loan debt. Really though, was it their fault I was unemployed? If I had simply used my engineering degree to get an engineering job instead of trying to become a writer, I would surely be well paid and capable of getting out of debt more quickly. But then again, I have always wanted to be happy and get paid for something I enjoy.

So there I was turning page after page of the *Chicago Times'* classified section, flicking the cap of my highlighter. With squinted eyes, I read the tiny text of one job description after another. My plan was to circle jobs I would enjoy. My first time through the job section, I ended up with no circles. Not even one. Either that meant I wouldn't enjoy doing anything, or maybe I would have to reconsider applying for engineering jobs. I decided to flip through the entire job section again.

"There must be something I would enjoy," I muttered to myself.

This time, I read each job description very carefully, in search of my dream job. About halfway through the page, I saw the phrase: "Are you looking for your dream job?" I smiled and continued reading: "Perfect Job for Recent College Grads who Love People. CALL TODAY!"

My first and only highlighted section in the classifieds motivated me to wake up early the next morning. I called the phone number from the job advertisement. After a brief phone interview, I was invited to the company's office later that day.

"This was an answer to my prayers," I thought to myself.

I ironed my best (and only) navy blue skirt suit. Then, I was off to drive to the north side of Chicago. Not really concerned about what the job entailed, I was determined to hear, "You're hired!"

During the interview, the managers explained how the position worked and more about the company. It was a promotional advertising company that sold party cruise tickets for yachts that sailed across Lake Michigan in downtown Chicago. After a series of typical interview questions, I was offered the job.

The vice president of the company said convincingly, "This will be an opportunity of a lifetime for you to earn some serious cash over this summer."

Since the position was commission only, the idea of not getting paid for my time and solely based on what I sold scared me a bit at first. But then I remembered ... I had nothing to lose!

Either the VP would be right or wrong. It was a 50/50 chance I was willing to take. I accepted the position as a Party Cruise Promoter aka door-to-door salesperson aka a solicitor—one of the best decisions I ever made!

After working there for only two weeks, I became the highest-paid party cruise salesperson, making over $1,000 per week, and sometimes close to $2,000. I figured out the key to selling the party cruise tickets was to understand the customer base. It was the men and women in beauty shops who loved to party. I would go into barbershops and hair salons and quickly rack up sales. The ongoing daily goal was to be able to come back to the office to literally ring this bell, which meant you sold at least 10 booklets of tickets. For each ticket booklet we sold, we made a commission of $20 plus bonuses. Selling 10 booklets in a day equated to making $200 per day, which would be over $1,000 for the week with bonuses included. On one of our bonus days, I sold 20 booklets which was $400, but the bonus was double my pay. I made $800 ... for the day! I'm telling you this was the easiest money I had ever made. For about 6 hours a day, I would go into local businesses and solicit away, selling party cruise tickets to anyone with cash, check, or credit card.

The day after I made $800, the boss challenged everyone in the office to sell 20 booklets with a bonus of doubling that week's pay check. I thrive off challenges. On that Super Bonus Day, I sold 20+ books again. My check that week was around $3,000. And since I made so much money in a single week, my boss was yelled at by the owner because the company actually lost money that week.

I absolutely loved my job. I had a team of my friends working with me, and I'd make a percentage of what they sold too. I even decided to create a uniform for my team. I purchased a bunch of fitted red tank tops and got a t-shirt company to embroider them with the slogan, "Ask Me About the Party Cruises" on the back of the shirt. My team of ladies would attend all the festival-type events like the Taste of Chicago. We did well selling tickets, especially to men because the tank tops were pure eye candy.

"Tell me about the party cruises!" guys would always shout to us.

And within seconds they would be pulling out their

wallets. Though, I have to say women were my most valued
customers because sometimes men would try to waste our time
by pretending to buy tickets in order to get our phone numbers.
I will forever be grateful for my party cruise sales job. As a
direct result of accepting that opportunity, I was able to save up
enough to move to Hollywood. I was very thankful to all of my
customers and the company.

My goal was to save $12,000 over the summer.
Although I made well over that amount, I spent a lot of it. How
much, you wonder?

Well, when September came around I only had $2,000.
Along with traveling to see friends over the summer, I primarily
spent the money on shopping sprees. I bought new clothes, a
cell phone and paid outrageous monthly cell bills for over usage.
All that money earned and spent! Making the money was so
easy. I didn't value it as much as I should have and spent it faster
than I earned it. With $2,000 to my name, I had two options:
1) Continue selling party cruise tickets for several months with
the purpose of trying to save another $12,000 and move to Los
Angeles later in the year or next year, or 2) Leave as planned but
with just the $2,000.

One afternoon, I had a heart-to-heart conversation with
my play cousin, who lived upstairs in our condo building. I told
Nikki if I stayed I might be tempted again to spend the money I
was trying to save to move to California.

She said to me with such faith, "Angie, if you don't go
now, you may never go."

The thought alone scared me. That evening I officially
decided to move to L.A. with $2,000 to my name.

First, I made a budget. Then, I found a place on
Craigslist to sublet until I could get a job and afford to secure a
permanent apartment. I also analyzed whether to fly there and
have my car shipped or drive. After much research, I learned
that driving was the most cost-efficient option. I asked a male
friend of mine to drive with me, and told him I would pay for
him to fly back to Chicago.

I was planning to leave in just a few days. One evening,
my mom came into my bedroom and leaned against the door.

"What are you doing?" she asked.

"Packing for Los Angeles," I said. "I'm leaving

this week."

"Wow, okay. You're really going through with this, huh?" she asked.

"Yep. If I don't pursue my dream, I'll always wonder ... what if?" I babbled. "I won't be happy unless I try."

My mother just smiled supportively, but also had a look that read, "I can't believe my only baby is leaving me."

Midweek rolled around, and the guy friend who was supposed to drive with me to L.A. backed out. Since I didn't have any other friends I would want to be in a car with for such a long road trip, I decided to drive by myself. Of course I had to keep my solo trip a secret from my mother because she would have totally freaked out.

On the day I planned to leave I went to a flower shop and bought a red rose. I then went home to pack my 1994 red Geo Tracker. I had my large desktop Macintosh computer, printer and all my summer clothes. Since I was moving to sunny California, I figured I didn't need any winter clothes, and if I did I could get them if I came back home to visit for Christmas. My jeep was packed to capacity, including the front passenger seat. It turned out to be beneficial my friend couldn't accompany me because there wouldn't have been room for him anyway.

So, this was it ... my last day living in Chicago and the beginning of my journey to breaking into Hollywood. It was about 5 P.M. on a Thursday. I was rushing to leave before my mother got home from work because if she knew I was driving to L.A. by myself she would have thwarted my plans to depart. I left the red rose and a note on her dresser. Next, I printed out Mapquest directions and said good-bye to my precious all-white cat, Sherrie Poo. Boy, did I love that cat. It was painful to say farewell. She meant more to me than any friend I had ever known. The sister I never had as an only child. She had been with me since I was eight years old. She was the best birthday gift my father ever gave me. As I was leaving the house, Sherrie gave me a warm hug. It was like she knew I was leaving for good to make another home for myself. I embraced her tightly and told her how much I loved her. Then, I looked around the house with a somber yet excited spirit, and locked the door for what I hoped would be the 'last' time.

As I sat in my Tracker, my heart was racing and my

adrenaline swiftly flowing through my entire body as I placed the key inside the ignition. I inhaled. Then, I exhaled and meditated in a moment of silence. I took one quick glance at all of my belongings for a final check. I shifted the gear from park into drive. Soon, I found myself cruising on the highway headed to Southern California.

THRee

Hollywood, Here I Come!

I was almost out of the state of Illinois, driving into Wisconsin as my cell phone rang. I glanced at it and of course "Mother Home" displayed on the screen.

"Hi mother! Please don't be mad," I blurted.

"Angela ... Marie ... Delk ... you come back home right now!" she demanded. "Where are you? Why are you driving by yourself? Pull over! I am going to meet you wherever you are and we can fly to L.A. together."

My mother went on and on. I could not even get a word in for at least 10 minutes. Finally, she gave me a chance to assure her that I was going to drive safely. I also promised to call her throughout the 36-hour trip. My mother calmed down a bit.

"Okay, where are you right now according to your map?" she asked.

"What map?" I squealed.

"Angie, you don't have a map?! Well, how in the world do you know where you are going?!" she asked adamantly.

"I printed Mapquest directions from the Internet," I said confidently. "I'll be fine."

My mother almost had a heart attack. She went ballistic and yelled at me for being a foolish and unsafe driver. Then, she kindly explained to me that along every freeway there will be signs stating the mile where I am located. She urged me to pay close attention to them and required I report back to her my mile number whenever we spoke on the phone. Once I told her my current mile number, she pinpointed my exact location within a few seconds. She sounded a bit relieved. My mother followed me throughout my entire road trip using her detailed U.S.

road map. She insisted I call her anytime I got lost or if I was bored and wanted to talk. She also stressed the importance of stopping at a hotel when I got tired. She didn't want me to have another run-off-the-road adventure like I did in college with my roommates when we drove to an out-of-state college basketball game.

To save my mother any further heartache, I neglected to mention I was determined not to stop until I had driven at least 24 hours. To make sure I stayed awake, every time I stopped to fill up my gas tank, I bought a cup of coffee and a bottle of Mountain Dew. I drank them both before the next gas stop. I was ridiculously alert at first. After a while, I became almost delirious and over-caffeinated.

Around the 25th hour, I saw a sign that read: "No Gas for the Next 100 Miles."

I thought to myself, "This must be a joke. There has to be a gas station within 100 miles!"

I completely disregarded the sign. Being a suburban girl, I just didn't believe there would not be any more gas stations along all of the exits. I was wrong! Suddenly, I was driving through Utah when I glanced at my tank. It was almost at E. I remember my father once told me if I am ever about to run out of gas, I should just stop or I can cause permanent damage to my car. So, I pulled along the emergency shoulder and parked. I sat there in complete disbelief. Here I was in the middle of practically nowhere with no map, no gas, no signal on my cell phone, and the sun was setting. Since I needed a miracle, the only thing I could think to do was pray.

Seconds later, when I lifted my head from saying "Amen," a silver car slowed down in front of my Tracker. I kid you not. A blond guy in his mid-20's walked toward my car. He didn't speak English very well; French was his native language. We communicated somewhat since I am proficient in French, but we mostly used hand gestures. Thankfully, he offered to take me to the next gas station, which was about 60 miles ahead. I was relieved at first until I approached his car to meet the passengers. There were three other men in their 20's who also didn't speak English. I had a major dilemma. Either I was going to try and hike 60 miles of hilly, desolate road in 80 degree weather or take up the guy's offer to ride with him and his friends. Before I made my decision, I quickly tried to use my cell phone again, hoping I would reach AAA or my mom, but to no avail. My phone would get a signal for only a few seconds at a time and then disconnect.

When I reached my mom, I quickly explained the situation and informed her that I was going to ride with four guys from Switzerland to the next gas station. She yelled and screamed at me until my cell phone disconnected our call, this time for good. I was no longer able to get any kind of signal. At this point, I didn't have a lot of time to make a decision. If I didn't ride with the guys, there was no telling how long I would be stuck roadside. And maybe someone crazy would stop and try to kidnap me or something worse, like in those Lifetime movies. I knew getting in the car with these guys could end badly as well. I could get raped and thrown into a ditch. After much thought, I came back to what I believed to be my reality and made the decision to let the guys take me to the next gas station. Why? Remember, their car pulled over just as I concluded my prayer. I figured it had to be God's answer. So, I surely wasn't going to be a fool and question it, even though I was quite nervous.

Wearing my little jean shorts and tank top, I squeezed into the backseat of the car with two other guys. I took a deep breath and said another quick prayer. Then, they asked me to move to the middle.

"No way! I'm not sitting between these two guys," I thought to myself.

I knew if I sat by the door I could jump out of the car if they tried any funny business. I started to rethink my decision once again.

"This is crazy. I'm crazy. What am I doing? What if God didn't send them to help me?" I asked myself.

Then, the driver explained as much as I could understand in French something about it being too uncomfortable for either of the guys to sit in the middle since they were taller than me. I eyed their very long, skinny legs, but I wasn't convinced. Finally, the driver sternly insisted I sit in the middle. He said if I did not do as they suggested, they would not take me because they were on a deadline and couldn't spend any more time with trying to help me. I took another deep breath,

said a quick prayer of protection, and scooched in between the
two guys.

It was silent in the car for several minutes. Then, they
started speaking in French and cracking jokes. I thought they
were laughing at me because they kept glancing my way.
The driver was personable and said he wanted to practice his
English. We talked about how they were headed to a soccer
game. I could barely keep my eyes open throughout the drive. I
was incredibly tired by now because I was about 24 hours into
my trip and still hadn't gotten a wink. Since I was in a car full
of guys, I tried to stay as awake as an owl. Although, a couple of
times I did drift off for a second or two, leaning my head on one
of the guy's shoulders. He kept shrugging me to wake up. Thank
God for that cause I certainly didn't want to fall asleep. After
about 60 miles, I saw the most relieving sight—a "Gas Station
Ahead" sign. As soon as the driver exited the freeway, I released
a sigh of relief. I couldn't believe it. Not only did the men not try
anything, but they also didn't ask to be compensated. We simply
waved our good-byes.

With sincere gratitude and delight, I thanked them in
French, "Merci beaucoup!"

By this time, my cell phone was working again and
I called my mother and told her I was fine. She said she was
praying so faithfully during the last hour, her heart almost burst
out of her chest. Again, my mother insisted I go to the nearest
airport. She was determined to meet me there.

"Mother, I only have 10 hours left before I get to
California. That won't be necessary. I'll be fine," I explained.

"Let me call you back. I need to buy a container of gas,
and then arrange a tow truck to drive me back to my car."

I called two places. Both quoted about $200. Since I
only had $2,000, I could not afford to spend $200 of it on a tow
truck. While standing inside a gas station, thinking to myself
and twiddling my thumbs, a casually dressed white man in his
50's approached me. He told me he overheard my conversation.

I thought to myself, "What a weirdo! He's telling me he
overheard the conversation I was having in my head?!"

He was looking at me just as strangely as I was looking
at him.

"You were talking to someone on the phone about

needing a tow truck ... right?" he questioned.

"Oh! Yes," I said and briefly explained my situation.

He replied, "I am the police chief of this town. My duty is your safety. I can take you back to you car, no problem at all."

"Yeah, right! You expect me to believe you?" I snickered, raising my brow.

He chuckled and said, "It's understandable for you to be cautious, but I am telling the truth."

"And if you were lying, you'd tell me?" I asked sarcastically.

"Outside are my wife and children in that sedan. Go ask them who I am," he insisted.

Surely there was no harm in asking. I walked outside and over to the car he pointed out. I spoke to a beautiful woman in the passenger seat. She told me he was indeed the police chief. She also introduced me to their two adorable young kids in the back seat. She said it wasn't safe for me to be driving alone and they would love to help me. I agreed. Glad I did.

They were the kindest family ever. The chief pumped gas into a plastic red gas can and also paid for it. Then, they drove me back to my car. The chief poured the gas in my tank. He told me how tired I looked and encouraged me to stop to sleep. I explained I had been driving for nearly 25 hours. He mentioned about an hour ahead I will approach a local college. He said his daughter lives on campus and she would be willing to let me sleep at her place for the night for free. He wrote down her number on the back of his business card. I told him my plan was to stay in a hotel. I figured I had met enough strangers for the day! The chief said I wouldn't be able to find a hotel because it was a big game weekend. He believed my best bet was his daughter's place. I had doubts but took the number, just the same, thanked him and waved good-bye to his family.

I was back on the road again. I drove for about another hour or so. When I arrived at the college town, I discovered the chief was right indeed. I stopped at four hotels, and none of them had rooms. Luckily, I found a motel. I walked to the front door at the same time as another man, but he was a step or two ahead of me. The front desk clerk addressed me first, probably because I'm a woman. I told him I wanted a room for the night. He said it was perfect timing because they only had one room left. The man standing next to me started yelling and cursing, saying he was first and he wanted the room.

"I don't want this crazy guy coming to my room trying to hurt me, so maybe I should let him have the room," I thought to myself.

But the clerk had already handed me the key, and I was pooped. I just said another silent prayer and went on to find my room. I felt like God was probably so tired of my prayers every other moment. I hoped He didn't think I was abusing Him.

After settling into my room, there was a knock on my door. It was the motel front desk clerk. He was a creepy-looking old man with missing teeth. I talked to him through the door. He said I left my wallet on the counter and waved it. I immediately opened the door and thanked him. I then plopped on the bed and fell fast asleep.

At about 7 A.M., I woke up feeling only slightly rested. I showered quickly and left the motel within about 25 minutes. When I got to my car, there was a piece of paper tucked under the windshield wiper. It was a hand written note that said, "You are a beautiful lady. Whatever you pursue, you will be successful. Good luck!"

I thought to myself, "Oh, that's sweet and weird at the same time. How does he know I'm pursuing something?"

I didn't recall telling him anything. Then again, I was so tired and delirious, there's no telling what I said to get that room. Although it was a sweet message, I still found it kind of strange. As I was driving out of the motel parking lot, the clerk waved to me with a grin. I politely smiled back.

So far, this had been the strangest trip ever. Once I was safely on the road again, I called my mother and kept her informed. She just couldn't believe all I had gone through within the last 24 hours. However, she and I both were very excited I was almost in California. I only had about five hours left.

Just as I reached Las Vegas, my engine check light came on. I decided to stop and get it checked out because I couldn't afford to get stranded—I was on a mission! I found a nearby Pep Boys. They said my engine was fine, but there seemed to be a problem with the light. Hoping to solve the problem, they reset my car battery. The check engine light remained on and as a result of the battery reset, my radio locked and would not turn on. The code to restart it was somewhere in my messy room back home. This was awful. I was going to be dreadfully bored without a radio or my John Grisham book tape, "A Time To Kill." I called my best friend Sarah. She told me to use the quiet time to think about my plan of action once I arrived in L.A. That's exactly what I did. I guess my radio malfunction was another blessing in disguise. Over the next few hours, I accomplished lots of productive thinking.

I have to admit, I was still kind of nervous to drive with the check engine light on. That fear went out the window when I stopped at a gas station to fill up my tank. A middle-aged couple saw my Illinois license plate; they had one too. They asked me what I was doing in Vegas.

I briefly told them my story and they said, "You go girl! We've been driving with a check engine light on for 10 years!"

Somehow their humorous spirit gave me the confidence to feel comfortable driving the last stretch of my cross-country road trip.

Finally, after 36 hours I saw the most magnificent sight ... the Hollywood sign! I can't tell you the feeling I received when I saw the sign. It was like all my emotions and excitement ran through my brain. I felt extraordinarily inspired. A few minutes later, I found the street of the apartment where I was going to be staying, and then phoned the subletter's boyfriend. In about 15 minutes, he met me at my car to give me the key. When I told my mother I was getting the key from a girl's boyfriend since she was out of town, my mom was worried once again. She couldn't believe I would be so trusting of strangers, especially since I was raised like most children and taught to avoid communication with strangers.

Although, I am also the same girl who once got in a car with an odd-looking old 'woman' who ended up being a man. He tried to kidnap me before I leaped out of his moving station wagon at seven years old. It was in my character to take occasional risks. However, my mother sometimes viewed me differently. My father, on the other hand, knew the real me. It was his adventurous streak I seemed to inherit. However, looking back at my crazy cross-country trip to Hollywood, I would forbid my children if they ever tried to do such a thing. As a new mother myself, I now realize my mother was in her right mind. I was the irrational one.

After I received the key from the subletter's boyfriend, I never saw him again. See, so there is something to be said about trusting your fellow citizen. Then again, there are indeed more dangerous consequences in taking certain risks in this day and age. I certainly would never recommend anyone travel the way I did. Driving over 24 hours straight, and then the rest of the 36-hour road trip on back to back days with little sleep was exhausting. My body was quite jittery from all of the coffee and Mountain Dew.

All that mattered now was the fact I was holding the key to my Hollywood apartment. I felt proud, excited and tired. I had to drive around a few blocks for almost 10 minutes before finding a metered spot. I parked on Hollywood Boulevard. After stretching, I grabbed a few of my possessions out of the car to take into my apartment.

While I was waiting to cross the street at the corner of Hollywood Blvd. and Whitley Ave., I thought to myself, "This sure doesn't look like the Hollywood I've seen on TV!"

It was evening time and there were transvestite prostitutes on the corner. The street itself looked old and dirty. Films and television shows definitely made Hollywood look more glitzy. But I didn't care. I was living in the city where dreams come true.

"Hollywood, here I am!" I screamed out loud as I walked up Whitley Avenue.

A random guy shouted back from his patio, "Congratulations!"

The inside of the apartment building was a New York-style, aged building. My studio was on the 7th floor. Inside the studio, I felt like I was on a movie set. There was a small kitchen, a living room with a loft-style bed and bathroom. The thing I found most odd was there were no curtains on any of the windows. I peered out the window and directly across the street was another building with a clear view into the apartment. I guess the young woman who was subletting her place to me was rather free-spirited—to get dressed and undressed with no window coverings.

After I toured my quaint studio, I plopped down on the stylish futon and took several deep breaths. I was beyond tired, but I couldn't imagine going to bed early on my first night in Hollywood. So, what's a girl to do? I hit the town!

FouR

Behind the Glitz n' Glam

Living in the heart of Hollywood was the best experience ever. This was my first time living in a major city by myself. I loved every minute of it. I arrived in Los Angeles on a Sunday. On my first night I went cruising around the city. I drove west on Sunset to see all the restaurants and clubs, then south down La Cienega, and then east on Melrose to see all of the shopping boutiques. Next, onto Highland, and then La Brea, where I saw a very long line for a place called Pink's, which I later discovered is the hot spot for delicious hot dogs.

On the way back to my apartment, heading north on La Brea, I noticed a long line outside of what appeared to be a club called the Guardian of Eden. I decided to check it out. I had nothing else to do and didn't know a single soul in Los Angeles. I went home to shower and as I was getting dressed, I danced around the curtainless apartment to my Janet Jackson CD. I curled my hair, put on a tad of makeup, which I rarely liked to wear. I slipped into a black, slinky but classy dress and into my black stilettos.

Even though the club was around the corner, I decided to drive with the rooftop to my Geo Tracker all the way down. It was exhilarating to feel the wind blowing in my hair.

As I approached the line to club, I was thinking to myself," There's no way I'm going to wait in this long line with these heels on."

I walked to the front of the line and approached the bouncer.

"How long will this line take? My heels are too high to wait forever," I complained.

He was trying to look serious and tough, but he couldn't help but crack a smile. He asked, "Are you by yourself?"

"Yep, and I just moved here from Chicago. I don't know anyone here."

"You don't know anyone at all? You shouldn't be going to clubs by yourself," he said.

"How else will I meet people?" I asked him.

"Go on in, sweetie."

"Thank you. I love L.A.!"

As I entered the club, I heard women waiting in line shouting angrily at the bouncer. I smirked to myself. Inside, it was relatively crowded. The music was vibrant, but no one was dancing. Almost everyone was just talking. It was different than nightclubs in Chicago, where wall flowers were rare. But here, I fit right in since I never danced at clubs.

Within a few minutes of being inside, a Hispanic man approached me and asked if he could buy me a drink. I politely declined and told him I didn't drink.

He said, "What about a coke or cranberry juice?"

"I don't drink soda either and the cranberry in clubs always tastes watered down," I said.

"Boy, you are hard to impress. Where are you from?" he asked.

"Chicago. I just moved here," I said.

"When?" he asked.

"Today!" I said.

"Today?" he replied.

"Yep, and I don't know anyone here," I said innocently.

He told me I really shouldn't tell anyone that because men are crazy here. He said he wasn't and that he was a teacher. He gave me his card and told me if I ever needed help with anything or wanted to hang out, to give him a call. I thought that was gracious of him. Either that or he had game. I asked him if he knew of a place where I could get a car radio fixed because I couldn't continue driving around L.A. without my radio. He couldn't believe I had driven all the way here from Chicago, and that I had to drive five hours without a radio. He told me to go to Al & Ed's Auto Sound and gave me the address. By this time, I was pretty tired and decided to leave. He offered to walk me to my car, so I agreed. I never called him or spoke to him again, but I was glad for his advice that evening.

The next afternoon, I drove to Al & Ed's. While I was there, I met a young man named Emerson. He was an assistant to a celebrity attorney. He offered to show me around town since I was new. He also mentioned I should be careful telling people I just moved here, which was funny because if I hadn't told him my spiel he would not have offered to show me around. Anyhow, I took him up on his offer. Instead of him picking me up, I decided to meet him because I didn't want it to seem like a date. We met in Santa Monica at the promenade and headed to a billiard club for a famous TV actress' birthday party. Afterward, Emerson asked me if I was tired. I wasn't, so he invited me to another party a friend of his was throwing at a club in Century City.

By this time, I had Emerson's last name, and at least I knew he wasn't crazy considering the famous people who knew him at the party. When he offered to drive me to the next club instead of taking two cars, I agreed. I can't remember much about the next party; it must not have been that spectacular. What I do remember is when we returned to the Santa Monica mall parking lot where my Geo tracker was parked, Emerson said he definitely wanted to take me out again because I was fun to be around. I felt the same way. He walked me to my car, gave me a quick hug, and told me to call him when I got home. When I got back to my place, I gave him a call while I was half sleep. That evening, I had accomplished meeting a trustworthy person who was fairly connected to the industry I wanted to be a part of in the near future. Of all the people I could have met, Emerson's friendship was a treasure.

Living it up in L.A., I spent several weeks partying, clubbing, dining, and of course, hanging out at the beach. Every day, I would drive to Venice and Santa Monica beaches to rollerblade and listen to music on my headphones. It was the most peaceful and inspiring activity. To see all the beauty of the sky and ocean was just breathtaking. For quite some time, I was having such a delightful vacation that I forgot my purpose for being in L.A. My dream was on the backburner, but not for long.

One Monday morning, I made a list of the tasks I needed to complete during the week. One of the important items I needed to accomplish was to schedule a meeting with Theresa, a prominent actress who was president of a production company. While in Chicago, I sent her a letter requesting an informational meeting. She replied with a letter instructing me to contact her office once I moved to Los Angeles. During my get-back-on-track week, I called Theresa several times and followed up with another letter. After a few days, I finally received a call from her office with a meeting date, but not with her. Instead, it was with another executive known as her right hand man. He worked very closely with her and oversaw the company's film division.

The purpose of the meeting was to see what type of movies they were looking to develop and to see if the script I had written fit their needs. This was my first industry meeting since arriving in L.A. I was excited about it. Even though I had heard sleazy stories about some Hollywood executives, I naively thought my meeting would be quite the opposite—little did I know.

On the morning of the meeting, I thought about what to wear. Since I was going to be meeting with a male executive, I chose professional ladylike attire to show a sense of confidence and pride as a business woman. I parked my car in the company's garage, and the security guard let me inside the building since my name was on a guest list. I felt important at first, but not for long. I ended up waiting in the reception area for about 15 or even 20 minutes before I was told to enter the office corridors. A handsome executive introduced himself, exuding a professional demeanor. I cordially addressed him, but he insisted I call him Jon. He was younger than I expected, about 32. I thought I would be meeting with someone closer to 50. Either way, it didn't change my excitement about the meeting nor my ability to stay focused.

The meeting lasted about 45 minutes. At first, Jon asked me how long I had been in California. We talked about L.A., Chicago and other lighthearted topics. I kept trying to bring up my script and writing, and he would just kind of dismiss the direction I tried to take the meeting. He kept bringing up social conversation. He asked if I was single or in a committed relationship, and also asked me to describe my ideal guy. I never wanted to seem rude. So I answered his questions, but attempted to bring the conversation back to my writing career. I tried to ask questions to learn more about the company and what they were looking for in terms of material.

Eventually, there came a moment when I became annoyed and frustrated. It was at that moment exactly Jon finally started to focus on business. It was like he was reading me so well. If I was cool with talking about personal stuff, he was cool with continuing to pry. But once he saw I was annoyed, he ended the conversation related to personal issues, at least for a little while. During the meeting, I did gain some valuable information about the company, how it started, and what they were looking for and future goals. Then, the remainder of the meeting went something like this:

Jon asked, "So, you like to write?"

"Yes! I love to write!" I replied.

"What types of things?" Jon asked.

"I have developed a strong interest in writing screenplays. But I have also written articles for newspapers and magazines, and poems that received awards," I said.

"Oh, really. What kind of poems?" Jon asked.

I hesitated a bit because I didn't want to talk about poetry. I wanted to talk about my screenplays. But again, I also didn't want to be rude so I replied, "Different topics."

"Like what? Do you have any memorized?" he inquired.

"No, I don't memorize them but I do have one with me," I said.

I just so happened to have a sample of a variety of my work, but as I was pulling out the poem, I thought to myself how it wasn't very smart for me to bring a love poem to a meeting with a guy. But whatever, it was too late. I was there, and it wasn't that serious.

I handed him the poem, which was written on white stationary with a red rose to the left with drops of water dripping off of the rose.

He read the poem out loud with expression. I was so embarrassed. It was a lovely poem, and nothing serious—just about sweet innocent love. But still, it was uncomfortable to be listening to my poem about love from this male executive.

After he finished the poem, he complimented me and said it was written very well. Then he asked, "Do you write about love a lot?"

"No. That is just one of many poems I've written. I

write about lots of things. Would you like to hear about the screenplay I would love for your company to read to consider?" I asked nervously.

"I'd like to hear more about your love poems. What inspires you, Angela? Do you fall in love a lot?"

Obviously, at this point, I was unnervingly uncomfortable. Jon's body language was very forward. He was leaning further onto his desk whereas earlier, he had been leaning back in his chair. He eyed me up and down from my legs to directly into my eyes. He was rather bold.

I replied, "No, I don't fall in love a lot. Actually Jon, I am in a relationship right now."

"Good for you. Is he your first?" he asked.

"My first boyfriend? No," I said.

"No, your first ..." he said hinting with his eyes.

"Um, I'm not sure what you mean by my first."

"Oh, so you like to play games as well as fall in love."

"What? No, I'm not playing a game," I said firmly.

"Is he the first person you've slept with?" Jon asked.

"No!" I said in an aggravated manner.

"Oh, so you do fall in love a lot ..." he implied.

"No, I am a virgin. I don't plan to sleep with him until after we get married," he said.

He started laughing hysterically.

"What?" I said awkwardly.

"You expect me to believe that?" he asked.

"You don't have to believe me, but I am telling you the truth. I have no reason to lie to you," I replied.

"Well, well, well, if you expect to move up in Hollywood, that's going to have to change," he said.

Speechless, I just looked at him with confusion.

"You know even my boss (the famous actress Theresa) had to work her way to the top. As a woman, you're going to have to bend the rules among other things to get ahead ..." he affirmed.

I absolutely could not believe what he was saying to me.

He continued, "If you really want to be successful ... well, let me just say every successful woman in L.A. has had *to give*, to get where they are today. You surely aren't going to be an exception."

At this point, I was furious. I couldn't believe my ears. I had to decide quickly how to respond, whether to seem offended, upset, humiliated, witty, or just laugh it off. I decided on a professional good-bye.

As I stood up with confidence, I said, "Well Jon, I have to get going. Thank you for your time."

"You're welcome. Think about what I said. I would love to read your script. You can e-mail it to me as soon as you get home. I'll read it and if I like it, I'll recommend to my boss that we buy it," he said earnestly as if he had not just grilled me inappropriately about my personal life.

"Thank you, but I am confident the script I have to offer is not what you are looking for, or should I say the script I have may be, but I am not willing to offer anything else aside from my script," I affirmed.

"That's what they all say. Think about it," he said.

"I have. Thanks, but no thanks. Good-bye, Jon."

I wish I could say I never heard from him again. He actually had the audacity to send me a follow-up e-mail requesting my script. For kicks, I came up with a few witty replies to his hilariously underlying e-mails and eventually we stopped communicating. I guess he got the hint. I was not going to sell my script in exchange for my soul, sex, or whatever it was he had in mind. I shake my head to this day when I think about that meeting. It was the first time I experienced some of what lies behind the glitz n' glam.

FiVe
Lights, Camera, Action! Plan

One Sunday evening, I was hanging out with a few friends. They were talking about not looking forward to going to work the next day. They lightheartedly joked about how I was a rich girl from Chicago living it up while pursuing my Hollywood dreams. At first I kind of went along with their perception of me. But I quickly realized in order to achieve my dream, I needed a support system and needed to network so I could get a J-O-B. I reminded them I came here with only $2,000 to my name, which was far from rich.

I tried to keep it real with my friends by letting them know I was actually running out of money and needed a job ASAP. They brainstormed possible ideas like bartending or waitressing. I knew my mother would kill me if she found out I was waiting tables with an engineering degree. I did have an interview coming up in a few weeks at NBC to work on their lot as a page, which is basically an entry-level position at a television studio. Otherwise, I did not have any other job prospects. One of my friends suggested signing up for temporary agencies so I could at least make some money while seeking a full-time job.

I'm always one who takes good advice when I hear it. I registered with several temp agencies, including Act 1, Apple One, Blaine & Associates, and a few others. I spent a lot of time in the Hollywood library using the Internet to search for jobs online through the various job sites such as Craigslist, Entertainment Careers, Journalism Jobs, Media Bistro and Showbiz Jobs.

One morning, Act 1 temp agency in Studio City called me for a job that paid $100 for the day; it was to be an audience

member in a talk show for a couple of hours. Getting paid to
watch a new daytime talk show sounded good to me. Later that
afternoon, I hopped into my Geo with the roof down to enjoy
the beautiful sunlight. The studio where the show was filming
was down the street from my apartment at Gower Studios
off Sunset. While waiting in the audience member line, I was
standing behind a punk rocker looking man who was wearing
mismatched shoes. He asked me if I was registered with a
calling service. I didn't have a clue what he was talking about.
He explained that if I registered with a background casting
service I could get paid almost twice as much than through the
temp agency. I definitely took note of his advice.

Being on my first TV show set was neat. Everything
seemed much smaller than how it appears on TV. In between the
scenes being taped, there was a man called the audience warmer
whose main job was to keep the audience excited and energized
whenever there was a break between shooting. He gave away
candy for answering TV trivia questions and also encouraged
the audience to practice their applause and cheers for the live
taping. He was very comical and comfortable in his own skin.
He cracked lots of jokes and even made fun of his job as the
audience warmer. He mentioned he moved to L.A. to become
a comedian and joked about how his current job was lame. I
thought what he did was similar to a professional comedian just
non-traditional.

Years later, during the time I was working on this book,
I just so happened to be watching *The View* as they introduced
the next guest. I recognized the guy's face, but I couldn't figure
out from where. He cracked a few jokes and that's when it
dawned on me he was the audience warmer from that talk show.
I turned up the volume on the television. I was very curious why
he was on *The View*. The hosts started talking about the movie,
"He's Just Not that into You," which was adapted from a book
he had written with one of his friends.

What a great breaking into Hollywood story: to see
someone I met when I first moved out here being interviewed on
"The View." During Greg Behrendt's interview, he mentioned
he never set out to write a book, and he is still trying to
excel in his comedy career. He was thankful to have written
a book. He was also excited it had been adapted into a movie.

He revealed that while this was a huge break for him, he was still pursuing his comedy career at full speed. The lesson to be learned is you never know how you will get your break in life. You may know how you'd like to receive your break, but you really never know who or what will actually break you into the industry you are pursuing. Also, you never really know how your actions specifically lead to the results you receive until after the fact.

Back to my journey ... while participating as an audience member of that talk show, I was sitting next to a petite, stylishly dressed young lady named Jasmine who was quite talkative. She told me how excited she was about her job interview tomorrow because she was tired of doing audience work for TV shows. I mentioned I was looking for a full-time or even part-time job. The job she was interviewing for tomorrow was to be a movie reviewer. Jasmine said they had several openings and that the group interview was open to the public. She encouraged me to attend. I was thankful to have met her.

The next day, I arrived at a beautiful, tall building on Wilshire Boulevard. I took the elevator up to the 7th floor. Inside the elevator were several guys that worked for a radio station. They exited on an earlier floor, which appeared to be an entire floor dedicated to the radio station. I figured this must be kind of a cool place to work if a radio station is in the same building. I exited the elevator and went to the company's waiting room. There were about 40 people applying for the movie reviewer positions. Soon after a female supervisor gave a brief description of the interview process and a test we had to take, Jasmine slipped inside. She waved to me, but sat near the door to be discrete since she arrived late. Once the supervisor left, Jasmine came and sat next to me. I was glad she made it in time because after a certain point, they stopped letting people inside to interview. I definitely wanted her to get one of the positions since she's the one who told me about the job.

First, everyone took the interview test. There were common sense questions, current affairs and also math and reading. I wasn't even really sure exactly what the position required. I just knew the title was a movie reviewer. The test seemed quite challenging for hiring people to review movies. After taking the test, the group of 40 had to wait in the room for scores to be calculated. A few people left while mumbling to themselves; they thought they had failed. It was odd for people to not even wait around to find out if they passed.

A few minutes later, the supervisor woman announced a list of about 15 names, including mine but not Jasmine's. The supervisor also called the name of the two people that had left. See! Goes to show you, never underestimate yourself. Those people basically fired themselves before they got hired—self-defeat at its finest.

"The names I just called you are all hired. If your name was not called, unfortunately, you did not pass the test. If you are really interested in working here, you can apply again in 6 months. Thanks for coming," said the supervisor.

I sat there happy for myself but sad for Jasmine, especially since she was pregnant and going to be a single mother.

"I'm glad you got the job, Angela. Everything happens for a reason," Jasmine said in a soft tone with a smile on her face.

"You'll find a better one. Don't worry. And thank you so much for telling me about it," I replied.

We hugged and after maybe two other times of hanging out with Jasmine, I never saw her again. Even though we had become acquaintances, she lived further south in L.A., so it was difficult for us to get together. There's a poem that says people come into your life for a season and a reason. I guess Jasmine came into my life to help me get my first part-time job. I was very grateful for her, and I hope she is doing okay now.

Now, let me tell you about the job. I was getting paid to watch new movies and complete a feedback form. Along with a group of about seven people, we'd sit in comfortable leather chairs and watch movies and trailers inside a conference room all day. At first, I thought it was the coolest job ever. Later, it became exhausting and made me not want to see movies for a while.

While working as a movie reviewer, I met Nikki, a savvy fashionista. Within a few weeks, we became good friends. Nikki's roommate, Holly, was a former beauty queen dating boxer Evander Holyfield. Holly wasn't much of a social butterfly, but she was always invited to high-end parties. She encouraged Nikki and I to take her place. We partied almost every night and every weekend— always on the VIP list. Clubs, house parties, bonfires at the beach, wrap parties, launch parties, celebrity birthday parties—you name it, we did it!

Sadly, toward the end of the summer Nikki decided it was too difficult to make it in L.A. Her dream was to become a successful fashion designer. She had recently graduated from Fashion Institute of Design and Merchandising in Downtown Los Angeles. Even though she majored in the field she was pursuing, she believed L.A. was all about connections and had nothing to do with talent. Personally, I just don't think she tried hard enough because we spent most of our time partying and enjoying L.A. Since we both weren't from here, we lived it up. I was sad when she moved back to Maryland. It's a shame we lost touch too.

By this time, I had been in L.A. about two months and still hadn't found a full-time job. I had a decent set of friends and a decent part-time job, but I still needed a decent full-time job that would allow me to support myself. My sublease was ending in four weeks, along with my dwindling $2K savings. I needed a new apartment and a way to afford the cost of living in L.A., which is beyond expensive. I would say overpriced. Now that I have managed to actually make it here for eight years, I feel proud to have survived in the most or second most expensive city to live in the US. (New York is number one according to Forbes magazine.)

As for my job search, I faxed, e-mailed and mailed over 50 resumes and cover letters. Even still, I never received a call for any interviews. I was getting a little nervous, but then I felt relieved when I remembered I had an upcoming interview at NBC. Since this was the only industry job I was able to get an interview for in L.A., I figured this must be the job I am going to get since no other options had come my way.

On the morning of my job interview with NBC, I received a phone call from my mother. She was frantic. I could barely make out what she was saying because I was busy getting dressed for my interview.

She was screaming into the phone, "Angela, where are you? Don't leave your house."

I thought she was joking because she knew this was an important day for me.

"Ha, ha, mom. I gotta go or I'm going to be late," I said.

"No. Angela, I'm not joking. Don't leave your house. The world trade center—oh my gosh," she said with panic in her voice.

I could not make out what she was saying because she was uttering incoherent phrases and talking very fast.

"Mother, is everything okay?" I asked.

"No! Angela the world trade center—oh my gosh ... turn on the TV. Don't leave your apartment. Stay inside all day," she said firmly.

"Mother, I don't know what's wrong with you. But please stop being dramatic. I gotta go. I have an interview and I can't be late," I said and hung up the phone.

My mother has always been a very passionate and dramatic person. I just took her call with a grain of salt and kept focused on my goal of getting a job.

I hopped into my Geo Tracker and headed to NBC studios. On my way I noticed the traffic was extremely light in the direction I was headed, which generally had the most traffic, yet the opposite side of the street was really crowded.

"Mmm, that's odd," I thought to myself before I shrugged it off.

My radio still wasn't working by the way. As I drove to my interview in silence, I said a prayer in my head that I'd get the job. When I pulled into the parking lot, it was completely empty. I double-checked my planner to make sure I had the right date and time, which I did: Tuesday, September 11.

I called my mother back and told her about the interview. She calmly explained what was happening. I wasn't really aware of the severity of the situation, but I did take her advice. I went over to Nikki's house and stayed there practically all day. In almost a state of disarray, we sobbed together, glued to the television with tears in our eyes. One of my best friends Arthur (who later became my husband) was from New York. I called him to make sure his family was okay and to make sure he wasn't visiting there. He and his family were all safe, thank God. Our country was distressed, but quickly united, and for that I am proud to be an American.

While there were many more important things going on in our country and in the lives of others during the last weeks of September, I was very depressed because I knew how difficult it would now be to get a job. A few days later, when things had somewhat settled, I called NBC, and they said they were very sorry, but my interview had been permanently cancelled. They were now on a hiring freeze.

I was still determined to make it happen for myself in Hollywood. I was determined to make Hollywood my home. I was determined to never go back to Chicago without first having made a living for myself. One evening, I made a plan, what I like to now call a Lights, Camera, Action Plan!

> *Lights.* Make some more friends. Network with industry professionals. Get to know the hot spots to hang out and party. Familiarize myself by driving around.

> *Camera.* Get a job. Get an apartment. Finish the final draft of my script. Sell my script.

> *Action.* Register with several more temp agencies. Apply for jobs online. Send letters out for informational meetings with TV/film writers and executives. Send query letters out about my script to agents, managers and film executives.

Immediately upon creation, my LCA! Plan was in full effect. People have always told me you can't plan everything in life. Of course you can. Things may not go according to your plan, but you can certainly plan it. My LCA! Plan gave me the foundation to sustain myself while pursuing my entertainment career.

Every year I have lived in Los Angeles, I have recreated a new LCA! Plan. Whenever I achieve a goal from the plan, I check it off the list. At the end of the year, it's always interesting to review my plan and compare it to the next year's plan.

Although I checked off many goals within my first plan, the ones I often felt were the most important had not yet come into fruition. I eventually started a new system of keeping track of daily positive things that happened to me in a journal. Then, I would use those good news items to tailor my plan on a weekly basis toward achieving the goals I felt were aligned with my God-given destiny. I was amazed at how much I was able to accomplish year to year, but also disappointed in the goals I was unable to achieve. I learned early on that my journey was not going to be as easy as I thought. Fortunately, I have always thrived upon challenges.

If you have a dream, whether it is entertainment related or not, I encourage you to create a LCA! Plan with your goals. Without a plan, you will be like the many actors, writers and directors that move to L.A. wondering aimlessly on a wish and a prayer. Even if you are religious, it takes more than prayer to make a dream come true.

Throughout my years living in Los Angeles, I have met a lot of Christian actors who say they are praying for God's favor. As a Christian myself, I am a firm believer in prayer but without your actions how can, or rather, why should God work the miracle for YOU? The most impressive actors whom I encountered when I worked as a talent agent were always ones who had daily, weekly, monthly and yearly goals encompassed in a career plan for their life. A LCA! Plan can give you an edge over others pursuing a similar dream.

Six

Inmate or Roommate?

My journey of breaking into Hollywood wouldn't be nearly as fun to share without reminiscing on my crazy roommate experiences. I was two weeks away from my sublease ending at my apartment. In order to afford an apartment by myself, I needed to find a full-time job ASAP. Another option was to find a comfortable roommate situation, which I could afford with my part-time movie reviewer job.

On my way from an interview I had in downtown L.A., I exited onto Sunset to head home to my studio. While waiting at a red light, this ridiculously blasting radio from the car parallel to mine caught my attention.

I looked over at the driver thinking like the 5-year-old Olsen twins from *Full House*, "How rude!"

The driver's radio was so loud, my ears started ringing.

After the end of a rap song, I heard the radio DJ announce, "If you are looking to network with business professionals, to grow your business or start your career in the entertainment industry, register today ... the Entertainment Business summit in Newport Beach."

My "how rude" thought transitioned into, "Maybe this is an answer to my prayer?!"

Since I didn't have Internet in my apartment, I went to the Hollywood library on Ivar. There, I registered online for the summit and purchased all the extra seminar tickets because I wanted to make sure I maximized my opportunities. My goal was to attend for the purpose of trying to secure a full-time job.

On the day of the summit, I decided to wear sleek black pants and a black baby t-shirt with "Noir Magazine" written in small hot pink letters. Noir was a lifestyle magazine I wrote for in college. I was one of the managing editors. It was founded by a friend of mine from the University of Michigan. The purpose of the publication was to provide an avenue for college women to express themselves through fashion, entertainment, health, business and education. I was involved in an entrepreneurial effort to launch the magazine nationwide, but only four issues ended up being published. The difficult part for us and many magazines was securing advertisers. At the time, the founder of Noir had moved to New York to attempt to launch it there while pursuing her modeling and acting career. I was focused on helping her while I was in L.A. pursuing my entertainment career. In any case, I wore the baby tee because it stood out. I hoped it would trigger people to inquire about the magazine, and eventually about me.

My other focus for attending this event was also to browse potential marriage material. Yep, that's right. Here I was headed to a business summit hoping to maybe find a husband. Just so you know, this stems directly from my parents, especially my mother. She always had me focused on finding a husband, and my father always said never date a man you can't marry. On my way to Newport Beach, I reminisced about the first day I arrived on my college campus. I fondly remember standing on the curbside of my University of Michigan dorm, South Quad, which was known as the athletes' dorm. As I gave my mother a hug and kiss good-bye, several handsome basketball and football players walked by flirting.

My mother noticed I pretty much ignored the guys, not flirting back at all. She very seriously said, "Angela, remember you are here for two reasons, and two reasons only."

I knew one reason was to graduate college, but I wasn't quite sure where she was going with the second reason.

My mother continued, "The first is to find a husband, the second is to graduate."

"Mother!" I laughed.

"In that order!" she declared as she drove off.

That comment stuck with me, unlike most things she has preached. On my way into the dorm, I pondered to myself what would make her say that particular order. Later, she told me that she valued an education more than a husband. She wanted to convey her point of how important it was for me to get married and have children. My mother and father definitely longed to be grandparents. As an only child, I was their only shot!

Finally after about an hour drive, I pulled into the hotel parking lot for the business summit. I parked my Tracker and headed inside the elegant hotel. I was thrilled to see an abundance of professionally dressed men leaving their luxury cars with the valet attendants. Many of the summit attendees had a persona of established business professionals. On the contrary, almost everyone I met was a struggling entrepreneur with a great idea or in the initial stages of launching a company. I later discovered that many of the men who had those expensive cars were still living in apartments or had roommates. That was kind of odd—to have such a high car payment and not even own a home. Not exactly marriage potentials ... at least not for me anyway.

I did have a lot of fun talking with different people and attending the various panel discussions. There were about 500 attendees at the summit. I scanned the entire group and didn't find any husband material. I did however meet a handful of professionals who I later befriended.

During one of the summit's activities, you had to give a shoulder massage to the person in front of you while the person behind you gave you a shoulder massage. This exercise felt creepy to me. The conference speaker claimed the whole point of it was to help you open up to the people around you. He placed a strong emphasis on the value of networking.

After that session, the 6' 4" man whose back I massaged approached me and introduced himself. David and I joked about how I massaged his arm since I couldn't reach his shoulders. We talked for a few minutes about the event, then about how I was new to L.A. Of course, I mentioned I was in need of securing an apartment. He kindly offered his condo. He said he and his roommate, Denise, were hardly ever there, so we would all get along fine. David gave me his contact information and urged me to call him if I did not find a place to live within the next few days.

My sublease was about to end in less than a week, so I called David. I explained my situation of how I didn't have a

full-time job, but was working to secure one. Since he knew
I could not afford a normal roommate payment, he offered a
rare deal.

"How about you pay $300 a month? You'll have your
own bedroom for the most part," he said.

"What do you mean by for the most part?" I asked.

"It's a two bedroom townhouse. Denise and I have the
bedrooms upstairs. Downstairs in our basement we have an
extra bed with a dresser. You can use the guest bathroom as
your bathroom, which has a shower," he explained.

"Okay, well what do you and your roommate do for a
living?" I asked.

I wanted to know the type of people I would have as my
potential roommates.

"We both work in sales and I'm rarely home. Neither is
she, so we'd be out of each other's hair," he said.

He continued his sales pitch. "Basically, there is no
other place in town where you are going to find a deal better
than what I'm offering. You can stay here a few months or as
long as it takes for you to get a decent full-time job, even if it
took a year. And you don't have to sign a lease. Whenever you
decided to leave is fine by us."

"Mmm, okay. Sounds good. Maybe a little too good.
Where do you live?" I asked.

"In the valley, in a safe neighborhood. Come by and
check it out, miss lady. You're going to like it," he declared.

"Alright, what's the address? I'll be there in a few
minutes," I said.

I jotted down the address then called my friend Nikki
to see if she would come with me. I picked her up from her
North Hollywood apartment, then made our way North on the
101 freeway. We exited Van Nuys Boulevard. Neither of us was
familiar with the area. We curiously observed the surroundings
as we drove down the street. The area seemed like a decent
suburb with lots of car dealerships and small businesses.
We noticed a lot of the buildings had Spanish billboards and
signs catering toward a Hispanic customer base. I knew L.A.
was known for having a diverse population and an increased
Hispanic population, but I had never really been exposed to it.
This area was very different than anything I had experienced

in the suburbs of Chicago and even in Hollywood. I was raised in Illinois suburbs and attended predominately white schools growing up. I was often the only black person in my class, and I don't recall there being any Hispanics. From 5th through 8th grade, I was the only black person in my whole school. Even so, I grew up learning to love all people.

My father was instrumental in making sure I did not judge others because of their ethnicity. He exposed me to different social and economic classes of people. This helped me realize how much I had in common with others, regardless of background. My father instilled in me a love for being an American. As I grew up, I embraced the fact I was as Lenny Kravitz sang it best—an American woman!

One of the reasons I have really grown to appreciate L.A. today is because of the diversity. It has been voted as one of our nation's most diverse cities. What I appreciate is that it's also very integrated. When I've been out at a club, I've seen everyone from White, Black, Asian, Hispanic, to Persian, Ethiopian, Jewish and many other ethnicities and cultures.

When we arrived at the townhouse in Van Nuys, Nikki seemed to be pleasantly surprised. I was lucky to have her as a friend because she was always honest and never held back her thoughts. If you don't have a friend like that, I encourage you to find one because it can be useful in pursuit of your Hollywood dream or whatever career you are pursuing.

We buzzed the apartment and went inside the complex. David met us in the courtyard and shook hands with Nikki. While we were outside he gave us a brief tour of the garage and secured entrances. He mentioned that his roommate didn't have a car, so I would be able to park in one of the unit's parking spaces. If she ever had company or borrowed a car, I would have to park on the street. He assured me it would be a rare situation, but noted there was plenty of street parking.

Finally, he brought us inside the townhouse. We toured all three levels. It was furnished very nicely. The first level had the living room, kitchen, den and full guest bathroom which would be mine. The house was very clean and neat. The upstairs level had the two bedrooms. David wouldn't take me into Denise's room because he said she is very particular about people going into her room when she is not present. I could understand that perspective. At the same time, if they were trying to rent out room space, I would think his roommate would give him permission to take me inside. I was only concerned with seeing the room to make sure it belonged to a woman. I didn't want to end up living with two guys.

He assured me 100% that his roommate was a woman. He said she is just very particular. I asked if I could just peek inside. He agreed but warned me it could be messy. It was quite junky, but smelled like a woman's room. There were a lot of different scents, smelling like air fresheners on top of perfume or fruity body sprays.

Next, David showed me where I would be staying if I chose to live there. We went down a long set of carpeted stairs into a small basement. There were no windows except a very small one at the top of the wall to reveal a little sunlight. There was a queen size bed and a dresser, and that was pretty much it besides a door, which led to the underground parking. It was exactly what you might expect for only $300 a month. He assured me I would have complete access to the first floor of the house, and he said I was welcome to use the refrigerator and living room with big screen TV. He said I could also invite friends over if I just gave a heads up so there wasn't ever any confusion. Everything was ideal.

I looked at Nikki for her thoughts.

"Angela, for $300, this is a steal. Plus, you're always on the go or hanging out at my house. Really, you just need a safe place to sleep," she replied.

I nodded in agreement. He offered me to think about it some more as we headed upstairs to his bedroom. There, we watched some TV and just talked about L.A. I guess he figured talking to me would make me more feel more comfortable and help me decide to live there. Before I let him know my decision, I silently said a quick prayer that the decision I was making to stay there was a good one. Then, I told David I would take the room for about three to six months, maybe longer. He told me that he and his roommate were fine with that arrangement and just wanted to help me out.

Just as we were about to leave, the floor underneath us started shaking, and then the walls. I didn't know what was going on. At first, I thought maybe a large truck was on the

street, causing the vibration. The shake continued a
little stronger.

Suddenly Nikki shouted, "An earthquake! Oh
my goodness!"

David was sitting on his bed very calmly. He said, "It's
just a small tremor."

"A tremor?!" I said.

And within seconds, it was over. I was still frightened. I
couldn't imagine what a real earthquake would be like. I didn't
give it too much thought either. I am sometimes superstitious,
and thought maybe God was telling me my decision to live here
was a shaky one. Looking back, it is probably exactly what He
was trying to tell me!

In any event, Nikki and I were ready to leave. I told
David that I would start moving in a couple days. As Nikki
and I entered my car from the underground garage, I noticed
it had been broken into. I left my rooftop down, so not exactly
a difficult break in. A few CDs were stolen and someone
rummaged through my Tracker. Even though nothing major
was stolen, I was a bit startled, especially since I had just
agreed to live here. I mean who steals from within such a
small underground parking lot?! Nikki encouraged me not to
think much of it. Certainly wasn't worth worrying over since
nothing major was stolen. She said if it was another resident
they wouldn't continue to steal once they see I live there. I
never kept anything important in my car anyway, but I was
glad it happened because it made me very conscious of my
surroundings whenever I parked in the garage from that
day forward.

Settling into my room at the townhouse didn't take
much. I thought of my time there as a temporary situation. I
pretty much lived out of my suitcases. A few days after moving
in, I finally met my female roommate, Denise. A bit on the
rough side, Denise was dressed in baggy clothes and indeed
lacked style. Our first opportunity to talk was when she asked
me for a ride to Target. Since she didn't have a car I didn't want
to make a habit of giving her a ride to places. Eventually, that
would lead to her trying to borrow my car. This was the first
time she asked me to take her somewhere so I agreed. I figured
this would be a perfect time to chat on the way there—a candid

chat indeed!

"How long have you been here in Los Angeles?"
I asked.

"Not long," Denise said.

"You're in sales right?" I asked.

"Yeah," she said.

"What kind?" I inquired.

"I run my own business," she said.

"Oh, really? That's neat. What kind of business?"
I asked.

"A massage parlor," Denise said.

"Oh, interesting. Where is it located?" I asked.

"I work from home," she said glancing at me for
my response.

For a moment, I didn't think much of it. But then it hit
me that her home is my home.

"Oh gosh, I hope she's not running some illegal
operation!" I was thinking.

A massage parlor inside a townhouse ... that did not
sound too professional, especially since I didn't see any massage
tables anywhere. So that meant these massages were taking
place in her room (on the bed I guess) or maybe they had been
taking place in my room. I was getting grossed out just thinking
about it.

She continued, "It was hard for me to find work after I
got out of prison, so I started my own thing."

I almost lost my breath for a moment.

"Did she just say prison?!" I asked myself.

I guess she could see the bewildered look on my face.
My family always says my eyes can never hide what I'm
thinking. I'm sure they were quite bulged.

"Don't worry, it wasn't for anything major," she said.

"How long were you there?" I asked.

"A couple years. I pulled a gun on my man 'cause he
tried to beat me," she said. "I shot at him ... not to kill him, just
to hurt'em. Teach him a lesson not to mess with me."

I just sort of nodded and decided to stop talking because
I wasn't sure if I was prepared to hear anymore. Good thing we
were parking. Once inside the Target, we decided to separate
and meet back in a half hour at the entrance. As soon as she was

far enough away, I immediately called Nikki on my cell phone. She flipped out.

"Prison?!" she yelled in my ear.

"I know ... shhh, don't say it so loud. You're making me nervous," I said.

"Nervous. Girl, you need to find a new place ASAP," she said.

"And that's not even the worse, she said she runs a massage parlor out of our place," I further shared with Nikki.

"What?! Oh no, girl get out of there! Massage parlor my butt. She is probably a prostitute and has sex with her so-called clients. I'm telling you now, start looking for a new place. I wish we had more room in our apartment, but you know we are tight with three people in a two-bedroom already," she said.

"You really think I need to move out?" I asked with such naivety.

"You can't be serious?" she asked. "Get out ASAP. Check in with me every day you stay there. Every day! So I know you are okay. Did you tell your mom?" she questioned.

"No way. She would have a heart attack. I want her to be around for when I get married someday," I joked.

All of a sudden I felt a tap on my shoulder while I was in the Target check-out line. I jumped. It was my roommate.

"Girl, you okay? It's just me," she said.

"Oh, I'm fine. My friend was telling something crazy," I said.

"I'll call you later," I said and hung up the phone.

After we both checked out, we drove back home. My crazy roommate continued telling me more and more about her life.

Then she randomly said, "I'm really a cool person, but I've been through a lot. I'm not crazy if that's what you're thinking."

"I don't think you're crazy," I said to her, but I thought to myself, "I think you are insane!"

Later that evening, I spoke to my guy roommate on my cell because he was out of town for business.

"David, why didn't you tell me Denise just got out of prison?" I asked, in a bit of a rage.

"Would you have stayed there?" he asked.

"Obviously not!" I said.

"Exactly. I knew you would not find a better offer, so I wanted to make sure you stayed here. I knew I would look after you like a big brother. She is a good person. She's not going to hurt you. I will make sure of that," he said.

I thought to myself, "Yeah, while he's miles away in San Francisco sure he's looking out for me here."

Even though I wanted to continue going off, I did want him to make sure nothing happened to me. Until I could get a new place, I needed to make the best of the situation. Once he apologized, I kindly accepted and never brought it up again.

After finding out about my roommate, I was always extremely conscious of my environment. When I took a shower, I made sure to lock the door and always paid attention to my belongings and so forth. I ended up living there for almost two months, and even though I was always on the search for a new place to live, it was hard to beat $300 a month.

All the time I had lived there, I never told my mother about my roommate drama. When she came to visit during my first Christmas in L.A., she visited my place. She said the townhouse was adequate, but she didn't like that I was living in a drafty basement room. While in town, she offered to let me stay at her hotel. I accepted with no hesitation. At the hotel, she said I was sleeping heavily and snoring loudly. I am not a snorer unless I am really tired or stressed. She now knew I wasn't sleeping well at my place. Staying at her hotel was the best sleep I had in a while. She encouraged me to look for a new place to stay where it wasn't so drafty. Whenever she gives me advice, I strive to abide by it.

I definitely needed to leave my current roommate situation, but I had succumbed to a comfortable routine. Aside from the crazy roommate sometimes eating my food and denying it, I never really had any major problems ... at first! After about a month, Denise and I had bonded in a light hearted way. She felt she could trust me. That's when she started divulging more information about herself and her crooked ways.

One time she asked me to take her to Ross, a discount outlet store like TJ Max or Marshalls. She said she had to return some items and said it's best if I wait in the car. I asked her why and she claimed she just didn't want to waste time and had to get back home. I thought it was a weird excuse, but anyhow I waited in the car. I was hoping she wasn't trying to rob the place and using me as her getaway car. After about 20 minutes, she came back in the car laughing hysterically.

"What's so funny?" I asked.

"They wouldn't let me get cash back so they gave me a gift card, but either way it's cool cause I can sell this card for money," she explained.

"Why wouldn't you just go buy clothes you like with it?" I asked innocently.

"I don't shop here. I just steal here," she explained.

"Huh?" I replied.

"Yeah, I steal a bunch of clothes and then return them. Stores used to give me cash back before I was in the slammer. Now, they give you store credit if you don't have a receipt. Makes my job a little bit harder cause I have to find a buyer for the gift card, but I'll still get my money," she said.

"You mean Ross' money? It is wrong to steal. Don't ask me to take you anywhere when you are committing a crime like this. I don't want any part of your lifestyle," I said firmly.

"Aw, man. You wanna get paid too? I'll give you a cut of what I sell the card for," she said.

I just shook my head in disgust and we drove silently on the way back home. Well, I was silent. She continued to chat away as if I was actually listening to her. The fact I was upset didn't seem to bother her at all. On top of this situation, another time I was in my room and she came in and asked if I could tell if this CD she was holding had been opened. I looked at the CD and it seemed completely sealed tight with plastic wrap. She went on to explain how she had removed the CD and was able to repackage it with a special plastic wrap machine. Her plan was to take the CD back to the store and return a bunch of empty CDs and get her cash back. They would never check inside the package since it was still sealed. I was fed up with hearing about all of her shenanigans.

I felt like I was living with an inmate rather than a roommate. Week after week, I started noticing more problems with her. She officially stopped being kind to me when I wouldn't take her anywhere in my car nor let her drive it. She became quite mean and rude. It was definitely time for me to

find a new place to live. There were two final draws. One was
when she revealed to me that her massage business was indeed
as my friend Nikki suggested more than just massages taking
place. I'll just leave that at that! The second final draw was when
Denise told me she was going to have some people over for a
small get together. I wasn't bothered at all. I was pretty much
never there, but this was the one evening I had decided to stay at
home because I think my friends were all busy or out of town.

New line. To avoid having to speak to any of her friends, I decided
to go to sleep early. Right after dinner, I showered and got ready
for bed before her guests arrived. After sleeping for two hours,
I had to use the restroom around 10 P.M. I went up the stairs to
my bathroom and smelled the most awful scent of smoke. I later
discovered it was weed, but I was that naive suburban girl who
was unable to identify drug smells. While holding my breath
to avoid the second-hand smoke, I quickly used the bathroom
then discretely headed toward the basement stairs. As I dashed
down the stairs, one of the guys mumbled something to me. I
tried to ignore him but he repeated himself louder. I didn't want
to seem rude or cause any drama because everyone seemed to
be drinking. I know things can unintentionally get out of hand
when you're not dealing with sober people. I spoke to the guy
and answered his unimportant question. Then, I said good night
and continued on to my room.

The drunk guy tried to follow me downstairs.
Denise immediately came to my defense and told him to leave
me alone.

"You're drunk, boy. Come back up here," she said.

He continued to follow me down the stairs. I just
ignored him.

She grabbed his arm and said sternly, "Seriously, leave
her alone. She doesn't want you. She's going to sleep. Leave my
roommate alone. Good night, Angela!"

"Good night. Thank you!" I shouted back.

I said my prayers and went to sleep for the night.
Wrapped tightly in my covers, I slept in a clean pair of
comfortable clothes to avoid wearing normal sleepwear around
unfamiliar people. Boy, am I sure glad I did that.

Around 2 A.M., while still sleeping I heard a loud voice
in my head that said "Wake up!"

Startled, I opened my eyes. I thought I was dreaming at first. At the foot of my bed was that same crazy drunk man. I was terrified and nervous. For a minute, I thought maybe Denise put him up to coming downstairs to my room. Then, I remembered she was protective of me earlier when he tried to bother me. Either way, I had to think quickly about what to do and say. I was scared because the music was so loud upstairs no one would hear me if I were to scream. God forbid if he were to try to rape me. I analyzed all this in a matter of seconds. My spirit told me to be strong, stern and fearless.

"What are you doing in my room? You need to go back upstairs," I said.

"No, I'm bored up there. I want to sleep with you. I'm tired. Your roommate sent me down here," he said. "Plus, I know you want me. I can tell you were fronting earlier. I know you want to sleep with me."

"Ugh, never. No, I do not. You are wrong. And you need to go back upstairs right now," I said.

He walked closer, much closer. Now, instead of standing at the foot of my bed, he was on the side of my bed, just a few inches away from me. He moved his hand to my covers.

Then he said, "Move over. I'm going to get in bed with you. I want you. And I know you want me."

My heart was beating fast. I wanted to break down in tears. I just kept thinking, "Please don't rape me, please don't."

But I never said that and tried not to sound scared when I spoke to him. I made a very conscience effort to be firm. I mean, this was my virginity we were talking about.

He leaned over as if he was about to get into the bed, hovering over me. I sat further up and grabbed the covers tightly.

"You need to leave right now. I mean right this minute. I am not joking. I do not want you. I want you to leave. You are drunk. You stink. And you need to leave, right now," I said.

He stared into my eyes, and I stared back as if I was fearless. He retreated. I wasn't sure why, but I knew I was safe. I felt a sense of comfort and confidence that he was going to leave me alone. Suddenly, I heard snickering in the stairs, and then sounds of people bursting out into laughter.

My roommate came down the stairs and said, "Man, get back up here. You are a punk. She set you straight."

"You set him up to this?" I asked my roommate.

"Why, what are you going to do?" asked Denise.

"Good night," I said and pulled the cover over my head. I was drained.

"Yeah, you better go to sleep," she said.

I heard footsteps going back up the stairs as Denise yelled random comments. A woman kept telling Denise to stop saying stupid stuff because she was drunk.

First thing in the morning I started packing. My safety was in jeopardy. Although the night turned out okay, it could have ended horribly. I did not know where I was going to move but I had to move as soon as possible. I did recall this older woman, Mrs. Baker, who I met on a television show set say she had an extra room I could rent. I searched for her number and gave her a call. I never thought to call her before because she lived in Torrance, which was further away from Hollywood than where I was living in Van Nuys. Luckily, Mrs. Baker answered her phone. She said the extra room was still vacant. I didn't tell her the details of my crazy roommate situation, but I did let her know I didn't feel safe living there anymore. She was warm and kind, a great aunt type of woman. She invited me to come by anytime that day. Since my friend Nikki was out of town, I drove to Torrance by myself and checked out Mrs. Baker's apartment. The neighborhood wasn't the best, but again I knew it would be a temporary living situation until I could get a steady paying full-time job.

Later that day, I moved out of my basement room without telling either of my old roommates. I left the key in David's room with a note saying I did not appreciate what had happened the night before while he was out of town. I instructed him to never contact me again. He tried calling me several times, but I never returned his calls. I almost never saw him again. Except two years later when I was at a restaurant in Bel Air with my best friends Sarah and Arthur. I noticed my ex guy roommate was sitting two tables away. I was hoping he wouldn't see me, or if he did maybe he wouldn't recognize me. I even tried to discretely change seats with Sarah so that my back would be facing him. A few minutes later, he approached the table with another guy.

"Angela, I am so sorry about what happened to you,"

he said.

"It's okay. It was years ago," I said.

He pointed to the man standing next to him and asked, "Does he look familiar?"

I glanced at the guy to see if he was a celebrity, and he wasn't. I did not recognize him at all.

I said, "No."

David announced, "He was the man at your bedside that night."

The man sort of smirked and said, "Miss Angela, I am so very sorry. I was really drunk that night."

"Obviously!" I replied.

The man reached for my hand as if he was going to shake it or kiss it.

"That won't be necessary," I said.

"I wish things could have turned out differently, but again I'm really sorry. Enjoy your dinner," said David.

He and the stalker man walked away. We didn't even give the conversation any further discussion at our table because Sarah and Arthur knew I did not want to relive my inmate-roommate drama. We continued our lovely dinner and enjoyed the after party among several celebrities. It was a fun evening.

SeVeN

Valley Girl

One of the most important elements to pursuing a career is getting established in a state and city that fits your personality and lifestyle. Many of the aspiring artistic professionals that move to Los Angeles don't ended up 'making it' because they aren't aligned with the pace of the city. It's more laid back than New York, which is more of an in your face city. New Yorkers are obvious with their pursuits and agenda. Los Angeles, as a city, has a much more secretive persona. Although most industry professionals in L.A. are always on the hustle, you wouldn't know it from looking at them or even hanging out with them. It's quite the opposite scene in N.Y.

In order to live a certain lifestyle in any major city, stable finances are a must, either as a permanent source of income like a full-time job or reliable freelance work. After living in Los Angeles for a few months, I met quite a few actors that suggested background acting for film, TV shows or commercials as a means to make ends meet. I took their advice and worked as an "extra" and ended up making decent money. I also gained knowledge about the production process. Sometimes the shoots were a lot of fun. The craft service snacks were tasty along with the catered lunches and dinners that varied from steak to spaghetti to gourmet meals. It was wonderful to eat gourmet food since I could seldom afford those types of meals on my baby shoestring budget.

Another cool part about doing extra work was seeing celebrity actors. One time I was on the set of the television series "Felicity." I always thought one of the actresses on the show, Tangi Miller, was so beautiful and talented. As an extra, it was interesting to watch her perform a graduation scene. She is an actress with a diverse range. Tangi was a role model for not only aspiring actors, but also black entertainment professionals. At the time, it was rare to see a black actress as part of the main cast of a TV show with a predominately white cast. Her role was ground-breaking, and she received an NAACP nomination for her work on the show. Ironically, years later I met Tangi when I was a more accomplished industry professional, and we developed a great business relationship which I discuss in a later chapter.

While doing extra work on the different TV and film sets, I found myself meeting lots of interesting characters. Most of the extras were aspiring actors, but I did connect with a few aspiring writers like myself. Some background actors had been doing this for over 10 years. They seemed to take pride in their work. The odd people I frequently met on set were pretty forthcoming with their weirdness and outlandish personalities. I never actually made friends with anyone that I was doing extra work with, but I did meet my next roommate, Mrs. Baker.

The first few months of living with her were fairly normal. I had my own bedroom and bathroom. While living there I was able to secure a full-time job as a receptionist/special assistant for a public relations firm that focused on promoting health issues using celebrities. I met clients such as Carnie Wilson, Montel Williams, and Larry King along with his wife.

Not only did I meet celebs from time to time at work, but it was also a great set up. I worked in front at the receptionist desk and it wasn't that busy of a company. I actually had down time to dedicate to my writing career. I wrote the first drafts for two of my screenplays. I didn't make a lot of money, but I saved what I could. I wanted to get a place of my own because I was tired of living with Mrs. Baker. She was starting to turn out to be quite the loon. I ended up having to get a new place much quicker than I had expected. To say the least, Mrs. Baker turned out to be even crazier than my last inmate-roommate. I literally could write a whole chapter about all I experienced living in her Torrance apartment, but a brief recap sums it best. Here's a list of her odd behavior:

    1. She kept a padlock on her door, leaving her man friend locked in there when I was in the apartment.

2. She stole my identity by getting my social security number from my paycheck stubs.

3. She sold my social security number to random people, and they opened up credit cards and multiple phone accounts in my name.

4. I received collect calls from prison on the private phone line in my room, particularly while I was home during the day on the weekends.

5. There were constant roaches in the kitchen and bathroom, so she was always spraying Raid.

6. She smoked weed more than my last roommate, even at 60+ years old.

The last draw with Mrs. Baker was when I received a call from Wells Fargo Bank at work. The banker verified my identity by asking several questions. Once I was able to confirm my identity, she inquired about a check.

"Angela, did you recently write a $2,000 check to anyone?" the banker asked.

"No, definitely not," I said.

"We didn't think so. Someone just tried to cash a $2,000 check using your checking account. Hold on. We are going to try and detain the person and call the police."

I stayed on the line for a while. A few minutes later, the banker returned.

"Ma'am, are you still there?"

"Yes, is everything okay? What's going on?" I asked.

"Well, we tried to detain the person but they left and must have sensed something was wrong when one of our bankers said we needed to verify the check," she said.

"I'm really confused. Can you explain to me what is going on?" I pleaded.

"Basically, a man tried to cash a check that was written to him and it had been signed by you. Well, your name was signed, but the bank teller noticed it was not the same signature on your account which she thought was odd," she said.

"I sign my checks and bank items differently than other

stuff. Whoever tried to get my signature from anything else, it would not be the same," I explained.

"Smart. Good thing," she replied.

"Also, there was a phone number written on the check with a 310 area code. I called to verify you had authorized the check, but the woman's voice didn't sound like you," she said.

"What do you mean? How would you know how I sound?" I asked.

"Prior to that call, I called the number on your account and got your voice-mail. The woman claiming to be you sounded dramatically different than your voice-mail greeting message. Our team suspected something was definitely wrong," she explained.

When I returned to my room that evening, I discovered that the phone number written on the check was the number to the private line in my room. I did not have that number listed on any of my accounts. I only used my voice-mail number which was a 323 area code for Hollywood. I immediately knew Mrs. Baker was leading this scheme.

However, when I looked around my room nothing seemed out of place. Then, I realized I wasn't sure how the room looked when I left for work in the morning. So the next day and days to follow, I purposely arranged my room different ways. Every night when I returned home from work, things had been rearranged. I confronted Mrs. Baker, and she denied ever being in my room. She said the only time she went in there was to clean it up because she said I was a slob. I thought that was a harsh comment to make, especially since the room was always left pretty clean. Even so, she berated me. It was obvious she felt threatened by me questioning her. Otherwise, why would she be so defensive if she had nothing to hide? With the help of my mother and my small savings, I was able to move out of the apartment within a couple of weeks.

Every day until I moved out, Mrs. Baker created drama. On the last day I was supposed to move, my stuff was piled outside the apartment door when I came home from work.

As soon as I entered inside, she held out her hand and said, "Key."

I gave her my apartment key without speaking. She then started going off at the mouth, telling me that I am lying about having a new apartment. She said I couldn't afford a better apartment since I worked as a stripper. Of course there was no truth to such a ridiculous claim. I didn't respond to anything Mrs. Baker said and just focused on packing my Tracker.

I was glad to be out of Mrs. Baker's cave and delighted to have my own place. I loved my quaint Valley apartment in Sherman Oaks. Finally, I had accomplished one of the major steps to surviving in Hollywood. I was renting my own apartment in a safe and clean building with no roommates. I was officially a Valley Girl!

eiGHT

To Whom It May Concern

From the time I decided to move to Los Angeles to the time I actually got my first industry job, it took over 100 cover letters and resume submissions. People often say the best way to get a job is through networking. This is true for any industry, but especially in Hollywood.

After I had been working for the public relations firm for a few months, they had to lay off several employees including me. I immediately filed for unemployment and signed up with several employment agencies. I started temping for various companies. A few weeks later, I received an e-mail from an entertainment industry group affiliated with an Episcopal church in Beverly Hills. Although I wasn't a member, I had been invited to the church by Arthur and signed up to receive their industry e-blasts. Occasionally, they e-blasted industry job notices and freelance opportunities. This particular blast announced an open position within the membership department of the National Academy of Recording Arts and Sciences (also known as the Recording Academy or the Grammys).

To submit for the job, I prepared my typical "To Whom It May Concern" cover letter and tailored my resume specifically for the membership assistant position. Then, I e-mailed it to the contact person. Within two weeks, I received a phone call from the human resources department at the Grammys. I was excited because this would be my very first interview for a professional, full-time job within the entertainment industry. They called me on a Monday and scheduled the interview for that Thursday.

On the morning of my interview, I woke up extra early to make sure I had plenty of time to get dressed. I ate a healthy power breakfast consisting of egg whites, crispy bacon and rye toast with strawberry jam. I browsed my suitcase of clothes to pick out an outfit. I only had a coat closet in my apartment, so I pretty much lived out of different suitcases and had a small set of drawers that came with the furnished studio. The decision of what to wear wasn't difficult since I only had one interview suit, but I still bothered to look. A girl can dream, can't she?!

The office was in Santa Monica, which I was familiar with from all the times I went to the beach when I was living in Hollywood. I had never actually seen the Grammy building, so I made sure to leave early in case I got lost. I hopped onto the 405 freeway and joined the crazy rush hour traffic heading south. From there, I took the 10 West and exited on Bundy. I made a few local street turns, and I was there. The building was pretty old looking. The Grammy symbol was embedded within the surrounding gate. It was interesting to think that one of Hollywood's biggest music events, The Grammys, was put on by the people working in this small, quaint building. Inside, the décor was modern and kind of hip, but nothing fancy. Even still, I felt cool to be interviewing for a position there. A few employees passed by the lobby where I was waiting. They were all dressed casually but trendy. I was excited about the interview. Finally, a man named Matt approached me and introduced himself as the membership director. We shook hands and went upstairs to his office.

About 20 minutes into the interview after he had asked me a host of questions, he said, "You would be perfect for this position ..."

Smiling, I gave him a curious look because he sounded hesitant.

He continued with his thought, "... But we just hired someone in-house."

I couldn't help but to sort of frown because I was thinking to myself, "Why in the world would you interview me for a position that has been filled?!"

Matt went on to say, "It isn't official yet, but today a decision was pretty much made to hire in-house. I still wanted to meet with you because you seemed like a great candidate and after meeting you, I am confident you will be a perfect fit for our organization."

"Who cares?! If there's no job, I can't fit in anywhere!" I thought to myself.

All I could hear coming out of Matt's mouth was "Blah, blah, blah ..."

The interview ended with him shaking my hand.

"It was a real pleasure to meet you, Angela. I will definitely pass your name to our team in-house. When another appropriate position opens up, you will be the first to be considered for it."

I took a quiet, deep breath and transitioned to my normal upbeat spirit.

"Thank you so much. I would really love to work here. I am glad we met. And yes, please do consider me for future positions," I replied.

"Definitely. Enjoy your day. I'm sure we'll meet again," he said.

Quickly snapping back into my frustrated mode, I thought to myself, "Yeah, right. Whatever!"

As soon as I got in my car, I called my best friend Sarah in Atlanta and then my mother in Chicago. I told them how I had just wasted my time interviewing for a non-existent job. Sarah and my mother are both positive people. Although they let me rant and even joined in with me, they encouraged me to hope for the best. My mother said if it was meant for me to work there, it would happen. She reminded me everything happens in God's timing. I agreed with that as a general principle, but sometimes it's hard to actually believe that when you are in the midst of a challenging situation. I talked with Sarah on my cell phone the whole way back home. (This was before holding the cell phone became against the law in California ... don't want to get a retroactive ticket!) By the time I reached my apartment, I was happy and confident again. It usually never takes me long to bounce out of sadness or disappointment.

The following week I was online submitting for jobs again. I still really wanted to work for the Grammys. I decided to do some research on their website. I skimmed their staff page to see who else I might be able to reach out to for a possible informational meeting with the hopes of landing a job there when one became available. I didn't believe they would keep my resume on file. The very idea of the membership director passing my information to others in the company sounded like ridiculous, wishful thinking.

While skimming the Grammy staff page, I came across an attractive and friendly looking executive named Andrea. I researched her name on Google to see what I could find, and a bunch of links came up with her name attached to a lot of famous people, mainly music artists and producers like Jimmy Jam.

You might be wondering if I moved out to L.A. to be a writer, why was I fascinated with trying to work at the Grammys? Although I can't sing or dance at all, I always found music and the business of it intriguing. Working at the Grammys could be a token entrance into the industry because of the exposure to famous and influential people. Also, the Recording Academy is a non-profit organization. The atmosphere seemed professional yet fun, casual and laid back, which is my preferred work environment. I found that people working for a non-profit organization often had more of a passion for their jobs than a passion for making money. After I finished researching the Grammy website, I wrote down Andrea's name and was about to begin drafting a letter to mail to her. Just then, the phone rang. You'll never guess who it was? No, not her. But close! It was the Grammys' HR department.

The woman on the phone said, "We have another opening that came up and you were highly recommended for this position by our membership director who previously interviewed you for another position."

She went on to give a description of the position and said I would be a special events assistant helping a vice president with planning Grammy events. She mentioned the position was a temporary, full-time position, but that it could lead to a permanent job. She asked if I was interested, and of course I said yes. Then, she asked if I was available to come in for an interview later that afternoon. I absolutely couldn't believe this was happening.

"Wow, I'll definitely have to thank the membership director if I get this job. He really meant what he said," I thought to myself.

I headed down to the Grammy building once again. The interview was on the first floor in a different office. I was escorted to wait inside a small meeting room for a few moments. Then, a young man and an attractive woman came in and greeted me with a handshake. I was a little startled at first because the woman looked familiar. I couldn't figure out why. Seconds later, I realized it was Andrea, the woman I had looked up on the website and was going to send a letter to try and meet with her. I so wanted to tell them the funny story of how I was just looking her up when human resources called, but I thought that might turn her off or make me seem kind of stalkerish. I kept it to myself until I got the job.

Yep, that's right—I got the job! My position as the special events assistant was perfect for my skill set. I was responsible for planning the Grammys' viewing party, bowling and golf tournaments, and I designed event gift baskets, among a host of other tasks. Through various Grammy events, I met a variety of people, from Jimmy Jam to Kanye West to Randy Spendlove to Randy Jackson to Dave Koz ... wait, those are all men, but I met tons of women too, just can't remember their names.

My job was amusing. I loved it. My boss Andrea was the nicest, most intelligent and helpful person that I had met in Los Angeles. I enjoyed working with her. As a mentor, Andrea gave me a plethora of advice about the industry.

The coolest thing about working for the Grammys was having access to the company's membership database. You had to sign a privacy policy stating you would never utilize the database for any purpose other than work. The database had every single member's contact information. The Grammy membership consisted of every established musician, singer, producer and other music professionals. The database included their home addresses, e-mails, phone numbers and contact information for their personal assistants, agents, managers. For kicks, I would look up people like Will Smith or Mariah Carey to see where they lived. I have to admit one time I looked up a few people and wrote down their address and even drove by to see if they lived in mansions. But with the surrounding landscaping, it was impossible to see their actual houses. Still, it was hilarious to know where famous people lived.

I loved having meetings with my boss. She traveled a lot, so when she was there it was rewarding to have her teach me. She also let me sit in on a lot of her conference calls with famous music artists. It was flat out one of the coolest jobs ever. All the members and board members whom I interacted with would treat me so nicely at events, especially when they found out I was Andrea's assistant. My job was only supposed to last for eight weeks but ended up getting extended for a couple more. Since I was unsure if it would become a full-time job, I had to start applying for jobs again.

A few days after submitting my resume to my various industry contacts, I received a call for an interview at Warner Bros. My meeting with the human resources director went well. Coincidentally, the weekend my boss Andrea was out of town, I received a job offer to be a second assistant for Steve Pearlman, a vice president at Warner Bros. Television. I really wanted to take the job because it would be my first studio job. The only downside was that it too was temporary with a possibility of becoming a full-time job. Also, the hours were a little weird from 11 A.M. to 8 P.M. I thought that was odd, but doable since I was a single woman with no husband or children yet. The pay was about $18 an hour, more than what I was currently making. Also, it was closer to where I lived. The Warner Bros. lot was in Burbank, and I was living in Sherman Oaks. My commute would be about 15 to 20 minutes.

The downside about leaving the Grammys was I didn't want to ruin the relationship I had established with Andrea. I didn't want her to think I was not loyal or committed. More importantly, I needed to know I had a job after the Grammy job ended in two weeks. When Warner Bros. offered me the job, they told me I needed to let them know in 24 hours. Yikes! My boss was still out of town and wasn't coming back for a few days. I thought about calling her, but I wasn't sure how to tell her over the phone. I chickened out and sent her an e-mail instead. I basically told her how much I loved working with her and how I wanted to stay, but I needed to know if I would be brought on full-time. She replied with a phone call and said she wouldn't be able to make that decision for a few weeks. She encouraged me to take the other job. And that's exactly what I did. I was grateful she understood my predicament. Later, I found out she didn't end up hiring anyone for several months. If I hadn't accepted the Warner Bros. job, I would have been unemployed and on the job hunt again.

When I left the Grammys I was still nervous my relationship with Andrea would change, but it didn't. It only got stronger. She still hired me for freelance assignments with the Grammys to design their celebrity baskets. After a few years, Andrea and I developed a friendship. She was directly responsible for helping me secure my first paid writing assignment for $25,000.

As for my job at Warner Bros., it wasn't exactly what I thought it would be like to work for a major entertainment company.

"I'm on a studio lot. I will learn so much and meet so many people and may be able to sell a script to them," I thought to myself.

I quickly learned that the Warner Bros. Television department and the film department (also known as the theatrical division) were separate entities on opposite ends of the company's lot. I was hired on as a temporary assistant specifically for TV pilot season. Warner Bros. Television was developing many new pilots, the most they had ever created. My primary job responsibilities included getting coffee, running errands, copying scripts, taking notes at meetings, organizing a tape library and covering the regular assistants' desks whenever they were on vacation or out sick. I was like the hand-me-down assistant, but it was all good. I actually had my own office and computer.

Well, let me not glamorize my office. There were no windows, and I was basically inside of a closet. It was actually the tape library. While working at Warner Bros. Television, I learned quickly that I did not want to work in television. I especially didn't want to work in development. The hours were long and the work seemed repetitive, at least from my short-lived observations. I was one who enjoyed variety.

Another thing I learned was how important networking was even for established stars. I had an opportunity to observe several casting sessions and pitch meetings. I recall a casting session when a famous actress from one of my favorite sitcoms of all times, "The Cosby Show," came in to audition for a lead role in a new sitcom. After the audition, the casting team and creative executives mentioned how she delivered the best performance but they wanted new blood. They ended up going with another actress. She wasn't really any more famous or talented. She got the role because of her relationship with the executive producers.

Another interesting experience at Warner Bros. was during staffing season when they were hiring staff writers for their sitcom and one-hour drama shows. My responsibility for the day was to drive the writers from one side of the lot to the other for their interview meetings. This was fun because I was able to be outdoors all day, driving around in the senior vice president's golf car, which was one of the fastest carts on the lot. It was kind of like riding go-karts sometimes. I remember getting passes for my friends to come onto the lot, and I would give a quick tour using the cart and ride through the different fictional towns they used to film scenes from movies and TV shows. I especially liked driving through Western town. I felt like I was in an old western movie.

The work environment at Warner Bros. was very competitive. Most of the assistants were extremely passionate and committed to their jobs. They were secretive with information and whenever I would ask them questions, they would always provide vague answers. It was almost like they were sworn into a secret assistants' society you had to be officially inducted into by getting a permanent assistant job, which wasn't my goal. Driving a golf cart on the lot, taking notes at meetings and getting coffee wasn't exactly the dream job I imagined out of college.

Most of the executives were also competitive like their assistants. Some were also quite rude and sharp. I did, however, find it interesting that the president of Warner Bros. TV, Peter Roth, was so polite. I remember when I got coffee for the executives and handed it to them during a meeting, they would simply ignore me. A few might mumble thank you. Mr. Roth was the total opposite. The first time I had to go into his office, I was quite nervous. I came in with the Starbucks drink he ordered, and his main assistant instructed me to go over to the table where he was having the meeting to hand him the coffee. I tipsy toed over there and gently placed the cup on the table next to him.

Mr. Roth was in the middle of listening to one of his

executives, and he actually motioned the executive to pause for a moment. Then, he turned toward me with direct eye contact and said, "Thank you!"

I smiled and said, "You are very welcome, sir."

Anytime I delivered coffee to him, he made an effort to acknowledge my presence, no matter how low I was on the totem pole. My direct boss, Steve Pearlman (a former Warner Bros. Vice President), was also very nice. He was married with children, and occasionally his wife would come by the office because she also worked for the company. She was in charge of the Warner Bros. Television Writing Workshop. My boss was indeed a man who valued his family and children. When I announced that I needed a few days off for a trip to Catalina Island because I was getting married (actually eloping), he did not hesitate at all to let me take the time off. He also got his main assistant to find out where I was staying in a casual manner. When Arthur and I arrived at our hotel, there was a huge, beautiful goody basket. At first, we thought it was from the hotel since we hadn't told any of our family or friends we were eloping.

When I saw my boss' name on the card, I thought, "Wow, how sweet!"

When I returned back to work the following week, I was then Angela Marie Hutchinson. This was a huge accomplishment to me, an important goal to check off my "To Do" list. Breaking into Hollywood with a family was one of my goals. I am thankful I was able to marry my best friend because he has been instrumental in my life and my career.

A few weeks before my job was supposed to end at Warner Bros., I started submitting my resume again. I received a phone call from MGM human resources to work in the home entertainment division as an editorial assistant. After two interviews, I was offered the job and a decent salary. I had a new job and a husband. Life was peachy.

At MGM, I was responsible for editing and sometimes writing copy for the DVD and VHS packaging, which included the taglines and story synopsis. It was a fun job, and I met a few friendly people. One of my co-workers, Michelle, became a really good friend for a period of my life. We had similar personalities and visions for our career goals, and she was also very smart and graduated from Stanford.

While working at MGM, I gained knowledge about the Home Entertainment industry, which is where majority of the money is made in producing films. It's not at the movie theaters, but with the DVD purchases and rentals where studios make their profit.

My integrity was tested repeatedly in Hollywood and even at my job at MGM. One afternoon, we were having a staff concept meeting about an R-rated stripper movie that MGM was releasing. Throughout the whole meeting, there were jokes made about sex, women and strippers, mostly by male employees. Although there were a few women who awkwardly tried to smile and laugh at their jokes to fit in, you could tell they were uncomfortable. I remember at one point they were discussing the graphic art for the DVD. One male employee suggested to make it a woman's breast and to create the DVD hole to resemble the nipple. I was completely quiet throughout the entire meeting. I could tell my boss was not happy that I was not contributing because usually I always had some of the best ideas.

One of my female supervisors said, "Angela, would you like to contribute to the meeting? You haven't said one thing."

I candidly said, "Actually, no, I would not like to participate in this meeting because this isn't a movie I would go see, nor do I support it even being made. I feel it is degrading to women and so is this meeting. I'm sorry. I am going to have to excuse myself."

I stood up and quickly exited the room, quite nervously. When I got to my desk, I took a deep breath and started cleaning off my desk and e-mail account. I just knew I would be fired, especially because a senior vice president of the department was running the meeting. The meeting continued for another half hour or so, and the whole time I was wondering if they were laughing or talking about me at all. I was worried if I would have a job. I felt bad for leaving the meeting, but I also felt I had to speak up and say something since none of the other women did.

As soon as I saw the conference room door swing open, my heart started beating rapidly. Within moments, the vice president of the department, who was running the meeting, headed toward my direction. My fingers started turning cold.

I immediately turned my head away toward my computer. I preferred not to draw any unnecessary attention to myself. Then, I could see him out the corner of my eye standing at my desk.

He said, "Angela?"

I looked up very nervous and raised my eye brows, "Yes?"

"I don't think we've met since you've worked here. It's a pleasure to meet you," he said as he reached out his hand.

We shook hands and I smiled awkwardly then squealed, "Nice to meet you too ... I'm really sorry I ..."

He cut me off and said, "It's nice to see some people still have morals. Good for you for standing up for what you believe in." He gave me a genuine smile and walked away.

I couldn't believe it. Was this really happening?! Did a vice president at MGM just give me kudos for leaving the meeting he was running?! My immediate supervisor smiled at me as she headed back into her office. I was shocked. I couldn't believe it. I exhaled all the air I was holding and almost felt light-headed. A few minutes later, I got an e-mail from my boss saying she'd like to see me in her office. Did I breathe too soon?! Oh no, here's where the firing comes in I was thinking. But it was quite the opposite meeting. We talked briefly about the incident. She then told me that I would now be responsible for our children and family projects. I was appreciative that this was the result of me speaking out on what I believed in because I could have been punished. Although I do remember later telling the story to an attorney, and he said if they fired me I could have sued the company and might have very well won.

NiNe

Surviving Hollywood

How does one survive in Hollywood with no family, no friends and only $2,000 to their name? Might sound like a daunting task, but when you aim for your destiny, you can achieve it by being focused and flexible. One of the most difficult aspects of breaking into Hollywood is staying focused on your goal while also being flexible enough to make the most of the opportunities that come your way, particularly when those opportunities don't appear to be aligned with your ultimate career objectives.

After working at MGM for a few months, it dawned on me that I had been in Los Angeles for about two years and although I had progressed in my career, I hadn't yet accomplished my dream. I remember eating at a Carrow's (similar to Denny's) in the Valley with my husband. We were talking about our life plans and dreams. I talked about how I didn't have time to write my screenplays. After working all day and evening, I was too tired to write at night. On the weekends, Arthur and I wanted to spend time together, as newlyweds do. Arthur suggested I quit my job, but he said the only way he would support me is if I were to treat my writing career like a full-time job. We once heard at an event that it takes about 10 years to break into the industry as a writer. This meant if I spent my day writing full-time, the time factor would reduce by half, give or take.

That evening, we created a plan of action. The first step was offering my resignation at MGM. I was nervous my bosses would not be very supportive of the reason why I was leaving because it wasn't like I had another job lined up. I was quitting my job, essentially, to write at home. Surprisingly, both my bosses were supportive and excited about me making the move into writing full-time. They even gave me a good-bye lunch and a congratulations card signed by the MGM Home Entertainment team.

  Around the same time I gave my resignation, my friend Michelle did as well. She nabbed a job at Paramount in development, which was more aligned with her producer aspirations. We stayed in touch even though we didn't work together anymore. Actually, we developed a stronger friendship because we both had the same passion and commitment to pursuing our industry goals.

  A few days after leaving my job, I relaxed and prepared for the transition. In less than a week, I was in full force. Arthur woke up at 6 A.M., and he returned home around 4 P.M. I wrote during the entire time he was at work. I had a few small breaks and took an hour lunch break. I didn't watch TV unless I was on break. I kept our apartment completely quiet, occasionally playing classical music. I also made sure to only check my e-mail during breaks. The only time I spent on the Internet was researching an answer to a scriptwriting question or to find background information I needed for a character, concept or scene.

  Three weeks into writing full-time, Arthur and I were informed that his grandfather on his father's side had died. This was indeed sad news, but it was combined with good news. Arthur received a letter from an attorney stating that his grandfather left him about $25,000 and that he would receive the check soon. Sure enough, we received the money in about a month or so. At the time, my mother thought we should have put a down payment on a house. In retrospect, that may have very well been a smart decision due to the market at that time, especially since we ended up buying our condo at the peak of the market in California.

  However, we decided to use his grandfather's inheritance money to replace my income instead of going into debt, which is how we were originally going to make do without me working. Otherwise, we would have had to charge up our credit cards. I was grateful my husband was supportive of my dream in every way. His commitment and passion for my dream was the backbone of my perseverance many times.

During the year I was fully committed to writing, I wrote three screenplays and performed several rewrites. I spent the first half of the year writing and the second half networking. I also researched professional writing organizations to join. I became a member of OBS (Organization of Black Screenwriters) and SWN (Scriptwriters Network). I also attended various workshops through Sherwood Oaks and other organizations where I met agents and studio execs. After being almost exhausted and brain frozen from attending a vast number of different writing workshops and expos, I realized I needed to really narrow my networking focus. I decided to just be a member of SWN and to only attend their events. I also continued from time to time to volunteer with Sherwood Oaks. Their events were expensive, but the founder would let me and others attend his events for free or at a discounted price by sending letters out to help him secure his speakers and panelists.

I really enjoyed attending the SWN meetings. The only thing I found odd was that in a room of, say, 75 writers at any given event, I was often the only black writer. I guess all of the black writers were affiliated with OBS and the white or all other writers were involved with SWN. However, I did not let that hinder me from becoming involved with SWN. In fact, it inspired me to take on a leadership position to serve the organization and its members. When an opportunity presented itself to join the board of directors as a volunteer coordinator, I jumped on it. I served on the board for about a year in this capacity. My primary responsibility was to recruit current members to perform tasks or to attend other organization's events to represent SWN with the hopes of recruiting new members. It was a gratifying position because I had the chance to interact with our members and learn more about their writing goals and experiences, which I used to help myself grow as a writer.

After serving on the board for a year, I was nominated and unanimously voted to become the president of the organization. I was the first African American president of SWN since the organization was founded in 1986. Below is the press release created by Elizarie public relations firm about my post.

***

Los Angeles, Calif. (Nov. 30, 2006) – Angela Marie
Hutchinson celebrates the completion of her year tenure as
president of the Los Angeles-based Scriptwriters Network
(SWN), a 501(c)(3) non-profit organization created by writers for
writers with over 400 active members. Hutchinson was the first
African American President since the volunteer organization
was founded in 1986. During her year of service, she provided
a strong support system to the board of directors and the
members-at-large. Hutchinson worked to ensure that the mission
statement of the Scriptwriters Network was consistently met, as
well as implemented new programs to increase membership and
promote diversity.

The Scriptwriters Network's mission is to serve its
members by enhancing their awareness of the realities of the
business, providing access and opportunity through alliances
with industry professionals, and furthering the cause and quality
of writing in the entertainment industry. In Hutchinson's initial
presidency proposal, she developed organizational objectives
to achieve during her term. "With the help and support of our
members, I was able to accomplish 85% of those goals along
with additional unplanned ones," says Hutchinson. She recruited
key committee chairs, including fundraising co-chairs and a
diversity outreach chair.

"A lot of my growth as a writer is due to SWN," said
Hutchinson. She has written four feature screenplays and was
selected as a 2005 IFP/FIND Project Involve Finalist for her
children's live-action screenplay. Throughout her presidency,
Hutchinson was invited to speak on various panels at film
festivals in Southwest Georgia, Memphis and Los Angeles.
Also, she implemented new diversity initiatives including
partnering the organization with ABC/Disney's Scholarship
Grant Program. As one of the SWN judges, she selected
two members as semi-finalists, Nissim Cohen and Lisa M.
Stewart. Hutchinson later nominated Stewart to join the board
of directors as an elected volunteer coordinator, which is the
position Hutchinson held prior to serving as president. "Angela
is an energetic and dynamic leader. Her passion, intelligence and
positive attitude was inspiring and took the Network to a whole
new level of productivity and creativity," says Stewart.

During the last board meeting, the board of directors expressed to Hutchinson their gratitude for her volunteer commitment and enthusiasm. "Angela has done an incredible job in her year as President. She's done some great things for the organization, and I've seen her grow tremendously as both a person and a leader throughout the year. She will be greatly missed," says Bill Lundy, SWN Chairman Emeritus.

At age 28, Hutchinson now has this accomplishment to add to her six years of experience in the entertainment industry. Moving forward, she will be seeking grants to expand Breaking into Hollywood, a 501(c)(3) non-profit organization she founded in May 2005. Also, Hutchinson will be collaborating on several writing projects and developing partnership ventures. Hutchinson will always appreciate SWN for igniting her scriptwriting career. She says, "I am truly honored to have had the opportunity to serve such an amazing organization."

The board of directors elected Joe Kondash as the next SWN president. "With Joe's leadership, a passionate board, active volunteers and the legacy of those who have previously served this organization, I am confident SWN will continue to equip talented individuals with the knowledge and ability to work as professional screenwriters," says Hutchinson.

As for the future of SWN, Hutchinson encourages the board of directors to focus on strengthening the foundation of SWN. "Since the founders are not involved in the daily administration of guiding the organization toward its original vision, it is important for board communication to embrace integrity while voicing a candid, yet respectful opinion, keeping in mind the sole purpose of servicing the members-at-large," explains Hutchinson. She also encourages each member to become an active volunteer. Hutchinson says, "Volunteering for the Scriptwriters Network is a great way for members to not only donate their time, but also serve an organization that wants to help them win that Emmy or Oscar!"

***

I learned a great deal about strategic planning and organization/association politics. It was indeed an experience for which I am very grateful. Running an organization like SWN prepared and inspired me to start my own organization, which I did immediately after I completed my one-year tenure.

Serving as president of the Scriptwriters Network provided me the opportunity to be a representative for Hollywood in other places outside of Los Angeles. I was able to encourage other writers nationwide to pursue their writing career. Shortly after my tenure as the SWN president, I obtained my first major writing assignment of $25,000 (which I am not able to comment much about because it was a ghostwriting assignment). With some of the money I made, my husband and I invested in one of my writing projects, a children's picture book, "Charm Kids". Along with publishing the book, I also created an online maze video game, song and animated music video. The book is available nationwide on Amazon and other retailers' websites, and the other franchised items can be viewed at *www. thecharmkids.com.*

Being president of the Scriptwriters Network also gave me some notoriety in the industry and outside of Los Angeles among the literary world. I was nominated for a Thespian Advocate award by the Memphis Black Writers Conferences and invited to teach a writing workshop in Memphis. Whenever I traveled to speak in another city, I realized just how much of a blessing it was to live in Los Angeles and to be right in the middle of Hollywood where it all happened. In Memphis and other cities, many aspiring writers were just clueless. Not because they weren't intelligent or educated, many were college graduates. They just weren't as exposed to the writing industry as one would be if they lived in Los Angeles or probably New York as well.

While in Memphis I had the opportunity to be interviewed by their ABC morning news show. The talk show hosts asked me a series of questions about the industry, which I later found out from those in the community that they found my answers enlightening. I was like a celebrity for the day in Memphis. The morning after my interview, as I went back to the Peabody Hotel where my workshop was going to take place, I was stopped by a couple of people because they had seen the interview on TV in the hotel. They told me it really inspired them to go after their dreams. I asked if they wanted to be actors or writers, and neither of them did. Even though they didn't necessarily have an interest in the entertainment industry, they had a dream of some kind and were inspired to go after it. That feedback alone made my trip worthwhile. I always felt part of my reason for being on earth was to help others discover their gifts, and then inspire them to achieve their dreams. Here is part of the transcript for my first TV interview:

***

Live at 9 with Reporters Alex Coleman & April Thompson

April: What opportunities are available behind the camera?
Angela: The power is in producing. The producer is the boss; the producer is the person who gets the actors, secures the financing and selects the director. The producer is the man or the woman. There are a lot of opportunities behind the camera.

Alex: What do producers and directors look for in these aspiring men and women who want to be behind the camera or a part of the movie-making process?
Angela: I think they look for passion. I think the number one thing is you have to have passion. Not just passion for the industry, but you also need to have an understanding of the industry. A person must be well-educated about the business. Having a passion and being proactive in your career. No one is just going to give you an opportunity to do whatever. You have to say, "I'm going to make it happen myself!" The ball is always in your court.

April: Do you have to get used to hearing the word no?
Angela: You have to get used to hearing the word, no. You're going to get a hundred million rejection letters. When submitting my scripts to different studios all you hear is no, no, no. But all you need is one, yes. All you need is ONE.

***

Memphis treated me with such love, and I look forward to going back there again someday to show my love to the community. At the end of the Memphis writing conference, there was a small awards ceremony held at a famous blues restaurant, and I was asked to host the event. I turned down the offer because I wanted to spend time talking with my friend Sarah. She had came down to Memphis to see me get the award and to hang out with me while I was there. She was always the adventurous friend who would show up wherever I traveled, to hang out with me so I wouldn't be bored. When I went to Georgia to speak, Sarah was there as well.

It was during my tenure as president of the Scriptwriters Network when I was invited to speak at the Southwest Georgia Film Festival in Colquitt. I received an all-expense-paid trip. I also receive a groovy, thank you gift bag since I didn't receive an honorarium like I did when I went to Memphis.

During the festival, I had an opportunity to learn about all of the film potential and opportunities in Southwest Georgia. The festival director arranged a tour of the local community. Also, we toured the sound stage lot, where the first sound stage was being built to prepare for movies being filmed there. It was at this conference where I met two industry professionals who I kept in touch with once going back to L.A.

One was a producer/actress/director named Sandra who was originally from Florida. After I spoke as a panelist during the writing workshop held at the Colquitt library, Sandra approached me after the panel discussion. She said I not only inspired her, but also provided her with useful advice. I appreciated her kind comments. Later that evening, I was in my hotel waiting in the lobby for the limo to pick me up for the festival's gala. I saw Sandra again and we exchanged contact information. We agreed to keep in touch, and certainly did. I later recruited her to serve on the board for my non-profit.

The other person I still keep in touch with from the trip is Joy Shannon, who is a director/writer and her brother-in-law is the prominent director Charles Burnett. I enjoyed meeting Joy because she had been in the industry for some time. She had a different perspective than I did. She was very much a realist. She is someone I respect because she has actually achieved notable directing credits and has had her share of struggles in the industry. I learned a lot from her advice and experiences. Since I am from a different generation and very much an idealist, I tried to provide her with a rejuvenated perspective about the industry, which hopefully encouraged her to continue her journey of breaking into and staying in Hollywood.

The other person I hung out with in Georgia, whom I met originally in L.A. at an entertainment expo, was director

Tim Greene from Philadelphia. He is full of life and energy and always a lot of fun to hang around because he has such a vibrant, entrepreneurial way of looking at the industry. He was also quite funny and cracked jokes in our limo ride with the other VIP guests, which included actor Glynn Turman who played the role of Colonel Bradford on one of my favorite TV shows, "A Different World."

In addition to the Georgia and Memphis speaking engagements, I was also invited to be a speaker at the Arizona Film Showcase in Phoenix. I was a VIP guest, and they paid for my flight along with my husband's since I had informed them we were celebrating our anniversary during the weekend of the festival. When we arrived, we met a couple of the other invited speakers. It was definitely an honor to participate. The festival was honoring actor and author Hill Harper, who is also a good friend and Harvard classmate of President Barack Obama. Harper campaigned on Obama's behalf during the 2008 presidential elections, particularly within the Hollywood community.

The previous year, the AZ Film Showcase honored comedian Wayne Brady. Since I was not quite on his level, it was an honor to be a special guest as one of the panelists and a presenter for the short film awards. Fellow panelists included Prodigal Sunn (from the Wu-tang Clan), who I eventually developed a business relationship with and signed on as a client when I worked as a talent agent. Also, I met Michael Davis, a prominent creator and entrepreneur involved in comics. Our panel focused on providing advice to youth on how to break into entertainment industry. I was the only female on the panel, so I made sure to answer the moderator's questions effectively and accurately. I wanted to represent women well and serve as a role model for the girls.

Hollywood is known as a boy's club, and sometimes it is difficult to hold one's ground and to gain respect from fellow male colleagues. Throughout my experiences I learned what worked and what didn't. When I met with different executives through informational meetings, the men always seemed to ask me a personal question or two, to see what kind of person I was, and to see if I would pick up on or take well to their underlying comments of questioning my morals and passion for the industry. They often tried to determine what I was willing to do to get to the top. I always conveyed the message that my plan to surviving in Hollywood is by taking a straight and narrow path. Climbing the ladder of success without losing my morals has always been a primary goal of mine, even if the climb ends up being up a mountain when it could have been a hill—a mountain view is astounding!

TeN

Reality Checks

Let's face it. In order to break into Hollywood, talent is not enough. You need an amazing support system and great connections, especially if you are not the daughter or son of a celebrity, and even then, networking is necessary. While in pursuit of my dreams, I received a reality check that changed my perspective on how to survive in Hollywood. When I say a reality check, I don't mean a new or enlightening perspective. I literally mean a reality check. I won $6,000 with my MGM friend Michelle and her friend Maria, who later became a good friend of mine. We competed as a team on the TBS reality show, "Cut to the Chase". We had to water-ski and swim in the ocean with potential sharks and other sea creatures.

A lot of industry professionals, particularly actors, stray away from reality TV because they don't feel they will be taken seriously. Some actors participated on reality TV shows as a way to make extra money. Although never a fan of watching reality TV, I became fascinated by the idea of being on a show to win money, like in a game show.

The way my friends and I got booked on "Cut to the Chase" is an interesting story. I wish this was a video book so I could show you our audition and the actual episode. It all started when I received an e-mail about a show looking for groups of adventurous and attractive friends who are willing to travel. I immediately thought of applying for the show with my friend, Michelle, because she is a beautiful Asian woman and very adventurous. At the time I couldn't think of an additional friend who could participate because my actor friends did not want to be on any reality show. I forwarded the e-mail to Michelle. She was ecstatic about it and said it looked like fun. She told me she had the perfect friend to make us an official group of three. Part of the requirement to be on the show was that you had to know your group of friends really well. You had to be real friends, not actors pretending to be friends. Regardless, Michelle and I both agreed this was something we should go after because we knew that it would be rare for them to find a group of young, fun women of different ethnicities who were good friends.

In order to act like we were good friends, Michelle had me and her friend Maria, a Spanish beauty, meet up at a Starbucks. This was the day before the audition. We spent several hours getting to know everything about each other. Maria was funny.

She asked, "Okay, so you're married. And what's your husband's name again?"

"Arthur," I replied.

"Okay yes, Arthur. He is so great!" she said with such sincerity even though she had obviously never met him.

We rehearsed over and over as if we were in the audition. We created all of these stories about how we traveled together to Vegas and how we threw parties all the time. One hilarious story we talked about was that we loved to take road trips. We came up with the idea that Maria and Michelle sang all these songs the whole way to keep me up as I drove. Then, we said one time we ran off the road. We felt kind of bad making up fake stories. At least they stemmed from our real-life experiences. I actually did run off the road on a trip with my best friend Sarah and some other college friends while headed to an out-of-state basketball game.

Another story we created for the audition was how I did not own a microwave because I am old-fashioned, so I made the best homemade popcorn. We added to the story that one time I almost burned down Michelle's apartment and had to call the fire department. We fabricated all these ridiculous stories and we practiced who would initiate each story. We figured we would ad lib along the way. Most of the stuff, although not true like I said, did have a truth related to each of our lives. For instances, I do actually prefer to make homemade popcorn and didn't have a microwave at my apartment. Not because I was old fashioned at all; that part of the story sounded charming. We knew that the casting directors were looking for entertaining and animated characters. We basically created a typecast personality for each of us. Michelle was the smart, spontaneous and sassy friend. Maria was the forgetful, outgoing and naïve foreign friend. I was supposed to be the All-American, rational, but overprotective mother of the group.

On the day of the audition, we met up again in the parking lot to briefly rehearse. We made sure we had the basic facts down, like each other's last names and birthdays, in case they asked. The audition was in Burbank in a small casting studio. We waited in the lobby, along with a few other groups of three guys and three girls. We knew that we had both potential teams beat because at the very least, we were more diverse looking friends. We nicknamed ourselves, "Charlie's Angels."

Once we entered the audition room, I remember thinking, "Oh, gosh, I forgot how to pronounce Maria's last name ... this is not good!"

Maria later said she was thinking "Oh, no. What is Angela's husband's name again? I know it starts with an A."

Since Michelle knew us both pretty well, she was thinking, "Oh, gosh, I'm sure they have forgotten everything. I hope we get through this!"

When the casting director came in the room, he just let us take over the audition and talk about ourselves as individuals, and then as a group of friends. That made it a lot easier because we would say things to trigger one another's memory of what we were supposed to be saying.

Michelle started and introduced us both and talked about how she and I met at work, and how she and Maria met in the airport. She went on to explain how she introduced me and Maria at a Starbucks, and we had remained friends ever since. Oddly enough, it eventually turned out to be true.

A few minutes into our audition, we had the casting director cracking up at all of our stories. At some point, we all started crying of laughter. Not so much because of the stories, but more so from ad-libbing. We knew if we had to repeat half of the stuff we said, we couldn't. It was hilarious. We were cracking up the whole time.

Afterwards, the casting director said, "This was the most fun interview I've ever done."

We responded with, "Does this mean we're going to be cast for the show?"

He explained that he wasn't the one who made the final decision. But he said the odds of us booking it were very high. We asked them if they had any other groups similar to us.

He said, "No, everyone was the same race and similar as friends. You guys seem special. Very unique and different."

When we first got the casting notice, we could have decided not to do it since we weren't true friends. We just knew that if we had been good friends, they would love us. And they did, indeed. A few weeks later, I received a phone call informing me that we had been selected for the show. We still weren't 100% clear on what that entailed, but we were very excited. We had another meeting with the casting director where he explained more about the show. Basically, we were going to be taken to a secret location that wouldn't be revealed until at the airport. Upon arriving at the destination, our cell phones and IDs would be taken by the production staff. They did not want us to have access to our cell phones because they wanted no outside communication with anyone unless supervised by staff or a camera man who would follow us. The goal of the show was for us to go through a series of physical and adventurous challenges like an obstacle course within a certain amount of time. If we completed the tasks, we would win the grand prize of $6,000.

On the day we were leaving for our reality TV show trip, I told my husband I would be gone for a few days, but I wasn't sure where I was going because they hadn't told us yet. Since they did ask us to bring passports, I figured we must be going out of the country. When we got to the airport, they worked so hard to make sure we didn't know where we were going. We didn't have to wear blind folds or anything, but they went to a lot of extreme measures. The three of us looked adorable in the airport; we were ready for our 15 minutes of reality fame. A lot of guys and security guards in the airport were making comments about how beautiful we were as friends and that they wanted to go where we were going. It was hilarious and definitely an ego booster, which was something we needed. Although we were all confident, we were pursuing difficult careers that from time to time made us question ourselves. It was relaxing to not focus on our careers and just enjoy living in the moment. The trip was a reality check experience for us in every sense of the word.

A few people in the airport called us Charlie's Angels, which was funny since that's what we had coined as our nickname. Several travelers looked at us like we were famous, probably because we kept our sunglasses on while in the airport. Also, we had two guys constantly following us from the show's staff. People may have thought they were our bodyguards. In a way, they were, but they were actually there to keep us from looking at the destination screens. The show's staff tried their best to make sure we didn't know where we were flying to for the show. Once we boarded the plane and the stewardess made the announcement, we realized we were on our way to Miami!

We all knew to pack swimsuits because they told us we would be participating in water activities. The flight was relaxing. We spent most of the time sleeping. We knew we had a busy day ahead of us. We wanted to be as relaxed and well-rested as possible. When we arrived, there was a driver holding a cardboard sign with our names on it, and she took us to the hotel. Upon arriving at the hotel, they took our cell phones and IDs. We thought that was kind of crazy because what would we do if there was an emergency situation and we needed them? I guess they figured since we were supervised by a production person at all times, we would be fine if anything happened.

On the morning of filming, we arrived at an unknown location. We had to wait in a van for about an hour or so until they were ready to begin shooting the show. As soon as we were instructed to come out of the van, the cameras started rolling. The host of the show introduced himself and gave us our first clue which was supposed to lead us to where to start the obstacle course. Even with a clue, we didn't have a clue as to what we should do. Eventually, we figured out the answer. We had to dash into the ocean in a nearby paddle boat. Then, we had to pedal the paddle boat about a half-mile into the ocean, where there was a very large inflated floating mountain. Once landing next to the mountain, we noticed a flag on top of the mountain that we needed to grab. As we helped each other out of the boat, Michelle's bikini top unraveled slightly. Maria and I quickly tied it back. We were on a clock, so we were moving as fast as we could. We knew that every minute counted.

We each had to climb to the top of the mountain. Once we all made it, we dived into the ocean. I was the last to dive because I had to put on my swimming cap. Since I don't have a perm like a lot of black women (my hair is pressed with a straightening comb), my hair would have transformed into my original hair texture of an afro, which is fine but just not my preferred hair style. The production crew was cracking up as I took my time putting on my swimming cap.

My teammates were laughing too as they shouted, "Hurry up!"

Finally, I dived into the ocean and was the last to swim to a small triangular float thing attached to a large speed boat. We strapped ourselves to the float. Once we gave the okay, they shouted to us via a bullhorn and said we will not be able to win the grand prize if any of us fell off the float. We signaled thumbs up to convey we were strapped and ready to go. Michelle was in front. Maria and I were on the sides. The boat went at full speed and we were sifting through the water. At first it wasn't that bad, but then, we could feel more water pressure beating against our bodies. We were shouting in pain from the water pressure, but we promised each other not to let go. Our arms and hands were so numb that we couldn't even tell we hadn't let go, except we could see we were still together. The boat shifted from side to side in circles and in different directions. We were flying through the air and then pouncing back onto the water. It was insane, and then, after several grueling minutes, Maria flew off the float. The production team stopped and came to pick us all up in a bigger boat. They told us no one had held on that long before during their other episodes. They said they went far past where we needed to make it to holding on because they wanted to catch one of us falling off for episode bloopers.

For the next challenge, they gave us a set of pink robes to stay dry. We had to ask a man inside of a staged blue Cadillac for a ride to find our next clue. We drove on the freeway, and they had a camera in the car behind us to film our ride to the next location. We arrived at a mansion that had a large swimming pool. The final challenge was to perform a synchronized-swimming routine we were taught in just a few seconds by an outlandish looking swim instructor they had cast. We ended up finishing the whole obstacle course in time. At the end, the host gave us a bunch of dollar bills to show we won the game, but we actually got our real $6,000 grand prize a few weeks later through their payroll department.

The show aired on TBS in between the commercials of the movie, "Fried Green Tomatoes." A lot of my friends and family saw it. We were glad we did it together because it bonded us as friends. Plus, we earned free money out of the whole ordeal. I have found that reality checks are a great way to make extra money while pursuing an entertainment career.

About a year before doing this show is when I actually received my first reality check. I was cast as part of the main cast of a teen court reality show, a pilot called "The Verdict" for MTV. It was executive produced by Leeza Gibbons. It was a weekend shoot. If the show got picked up, we would actually be series regulars. The show covered a diverse range of controversial topics. There was a judge and a set of three other jurors who had distinctive personalities.

The audition process for the show was pretty long and drawn out. First, I had an interview with a casting director about my point of views about life, love, political views and religious beliefs. I was also asked about my dating views and my preferred political party. They also took note of my thoughts on homosexuality, drugs and our society's laws. I suppose I must have passed the first round because I was invited back to another audition. I was told the second audition would be a sample of how the show format would be, so I was required to debate on a variety of topics.

They gave me a list of how I could prepare. It didn't seem helpful, so I decided to wing it. The funny thing was that weekend I was driving down La Cienega with Arthur (who at the time was just a friend), and we stopped at a light right by the Beverly Center. I happened to look to my left and saw a former college classmate, Steven, who was in my French class at the University of Michigan.

I rolled down my window, waving frantically and I shouted, "Hey! Remember me from Michigan?"

"Yeah, Angela! You were in my French class. How are you?" he said.

I was kind of surprised he remembered me. We chatted for the duration of the red light and even as the light turned green.

A few days later, I approached the small studio where the audition for "The Verdict" was taking place. There, standing in the waiting area was Steven! We started cracking up.

"You're here for this too?" he asked.

"Yep. That's so funny we are seeing each other twice just a few days apart!" I said.

"Heck yeah, what are the odds?!" he said. "We are going to take these people out!"

"Go Blue!" I replied.

He and I were lucky because we were able to watch the group before us do their audition. The casting team seemed to have selected a similar looking group as the one in the waiting area, in terms of balancing the male to female ratio and ethnicity. As we listened to the other group debate, we observed the casting team and made a mental note of what they seemed to be looking for in the show's cast.

Steven and I talked to each other about our various points of view to try and figure out why they had selected us. He was more liberal, while I was more conservative. So we both agreed we had to really play up our opposite viewpoints. We agreed to attack each other, but in the end there would be no hard feelings. It was definitely fate that allowed the pieces to fit like they did because no one else was able to genuinely vibe off of each other.

When it was our group's turn, they had the other groups stay to watch us debate. As they tossed out different questions, we talked about our opinions. They asked us to state what we would decide if this were a case we had to provide a verdict. It was so much fun.

Steven and I went at each other like we totally couldn't stand one another. During one of the questions, we actually agreed and acted like such a cohesive team, giving each other high-fives. After we finished our debate, the casting team switched out two of our group members and put in two other people from one of the other groups. They gave us another controversial topic, and we debated again.

Then, they had Steven and I step out while another two

people replaced us. This switching of different people went on for about two hours. After each session some people were let go. By the end of the evening, I was exhausted. I had participated in almost every debate, and so had Steven.

A few days later, I received a phone call saying I was selected as a semi-finalist to be on the cast. The decision would be made during a sample live taping, which we would be paid to film. The pay was about $800—not bad for a day's work. The live set was in downtown Los Angeles. As I drove past the hotel-like building we were going to be filming in, I noticed a full production crew and equipment. Since it was still an audition, I didn't expect there to be so many production people there. I was a little nervous because it was like I was having a live audition. I was thinking about how embarrassed I would feel if I was not selected to be on the cast after having come this far, and to be rejected in front of the whole production team would feel awful.

There was even a make-up crew and everything. I spent about an hour in hair and make-up, which was fun. The make-up artists tried to convince me to pluck a few little hairs I have on my chin, but I wouldn't let them. We had a whole debate about it, but in the end I held to my ground. My current hair stylist is still trying to convince me to remove them! They also tried to get me to pluck my eyebrows, but I have always loved the natural shape of my brows and have never had them plucked. I surely wasn't going to start now. After hair and make-up, it was time for the live debate audition. I had been grouped again with my Michigan friend and two other people. There was one other group there as well.

Each group debated two cases. Then, we took a break and had to wait around for the producing team to make their decision on who was going to be cast for the show. After about an hour, Steven and I were notified we had been selected as the cast members, along with two people from the other group. One of the girls was very passionate and wild (a bit of a potty mouth). The other guy seemed to be very neutral and laid back. He was an aspiring comedian and the nephew of a famous comedian. I felt bad for the rejected group because they looked sad. They were asked by the production team to remain for the duration of the taping to be our stand-ins. I was surprised they stayed.

We filmed several episodes that day, and each of us had

our own make-up person and chair with our name taped on it. In between every take, the make-up and wardrobe women would approach me and the other girl to make sure we were in order. Although doing the show was very fun, it became tiring after a while. It was hot with all the bright camera lights on us while we were filming.

The next day on set, we met and spent time with Leeza Gibbons. I was thrilled she was producing the show. I have always loved her as a journalist and celebrity personality. She was so beautiful and pleasant. In between one of the takes for one of the more emotional cases, she approached me off camera and said she really respected me for speaking up on my point of view. She said she liked my strong family values. I figured she must have been conservative herself to like my points of view, or maybe she said that to be comforting since my fellow jurors were quite harsh on me during that episode. She also gave me a few camera tricks to appear thinner, like how to position my legs instead of crossing them. I felt honored she had selected me to be a part of the cast.

During the next day of filming we were introduced to MTV executives. Since it was a pilot, it was up to these execs to make the decision whether to greenlight the show or not. The crew and cast were courteous to them and expressed gratitude to MTV for considering the project. The second day of filming was quite interesting. The producing team obviously had a vision for the show. In other words, they had cast us because we represented a certain view point or character in society. They wanted to make sure we stuck within that character and never deviated.

For instance, even though I may not agree with having an abortion for myself, they might have preferred me to say I didn't believe in abortions at all and that I hate any woman who does that, even though that was certainly not my belief. Sometimes, they held up signs for us if they wanted us to convey a certain message. Whenever the production team held up signs with lines for the comedian juror, he would always say the line.

We also had to tape scenes individually. We spoke into a camera about our fellow jurors or the topic at hand, and the camera person would try to instigate a situation to try and cause me to say something mean about a fellow juror. I am assuming it was for their editing purposes. They wanted to paint a certain picture of each of us. But I was hip to what they were doing early on, although I played pretty dumb. Sometimes when they held up signs for me, I would read them and other times, if I didn't agree with what the sign said or just didn't want to say what they wanted, I wouldn't. And I would try to be careful what I said about my fellow jurors because I didn't want to appear to the viewers like I was a backstabber or jerk.

During a very heated case, the wild juror with a potty mouth went off on me. Then the cameramen zoomed in so close to my face as if I was going to go off on her. But I was very controlled. When the cameras cut, she broke out into tears and said she was sorry for calling me out of my name. Later, I found out she had a lot of personal issues she was dealing with in her life, which is probably one of the reasons why they cast her for the show. She was a loose cannon, which made for good TV.

Later that evening, we filmed the intro to the show on the rooftop of the skyscraper building we had been filming in all day. There was a still photographer taking group and individual photos of the cast. We had to pose and do various walks around the roof top for the opening. It was very repetitive at times, but still fun. Leeza snapped lots of pictures with us, and she joked around a lot when she could tell we were tired. We definitely bonded as a cast. The show didn't get picked up by MTV. But it was still an experience I cherish, and a reality check I enjoyed spending.

eLeVeN
Making of the A-list

When Hollywood references A-list actors, producers or directors, they are typically referring to the top celebrity talent who have a recognizable name across the U.S., and often overseas. These prominent individuals can get a film financed, greenlighted and also cause a huge audience to support the film.

The B-list refers to talent that have somewhat of a name. They may have worked in the industry for years and have a substantial list of credits. Typically, they are the non-award winners, although some B-list actors have won notable awards.

When I worked as a talent agent, people often asked me if I repped anybody famous and I would say, "No, I represent C-list actors."

If the person asking wasn't in the industry, they had a curious look on their face. If they were an industry professional, they would laugh as if I was making a rude joke. I think it has a positive meaning because I'd rather have a client on the C-list, than a client on no list. I considered the C-list to be working actors. Those actors who are making a living from acting, but you have never heard of their names. They may not have a lot of IMDb (Internet Movie Database) credits because they are booking lots of national commercials, which aren't typically credited on IMDb. C-listers are the ones whose faces you may recognize from an insurance or Popeye's Chicken commercial.

Do you recognize the name Paul Marcarelli? I'm sure no one reading this book will. However, I know everyone knows his face. He's famous for the "Can you hear me now?" line. To some, he might be considered a C-list actor. I think he's more a B-lister because although no one knows his name, almost everyone recognizes his face as the Verizon guy. He might even be making more money than some borderline A-listers.

I view the A-listers in my life as those individuals who have been supportive of my career and a part of Angela's team. Making the A-list is a daunting task because it sometimes takes years to develop relationships with good friends and mentors. It even takes time to establish which family members are truly on your side and are passionate about supporting you or rooting you on as you pursue your goals. In the dedication page of this book, I acknowledge my A-list team. I'd like to take this chapter to introduce a few of them and their specific contributions to my entertainment career and life as a whole.

Some of my A-listers came into my life by choice. Others not so much, like my parents. Throughout my life, my mother and father have always encouraged me to go after my dreams whatever they were at the time. My father is a dreamer. My mother is a realist. It's a great parent combination and probably contributed to my viewpoint of the world as a registered Independent.

Since moving to California, my mother has spent countless hours on the phone with me, helping me strategize a plan for my career, brainstorming ideas or just being a listening ear for whatever I was facing at the time. If she had a dollar for every minute she spent on the phone with me, she would be a millionaire! She is like a walking encyclopedia and bible. With all of her life experiences and lessons she has learned, she uses them to help me. My parents divorced when I was 10. Although I am close to my father, I don't talk to him as much as I would like, and not nearly as much as I do with my mom. Whenever we do chat, he offers wise advice. One time I was telling him how hard it is to sell a screenplay and how difficult it is to write a great movie that executives want to buy.

My father said, "It's all about networking. If people meet you, they will like you. They will want to be in business with you and will buy whatever you sell them. Get out there and network."

I replied, "Daddy, it's not just about networking!"

"Yes, it is. Bad movies are made every day. How many have you seen?" he asked.

I suppose he had a point to some degree. At that time,

I was focused on making my screenplays perfect. My father's advice triggered me to really go crazy with meeting people. I spent several months sending letters to industry executives, requesting to meet with them. I also attended various events and workshops. My obsessive personality made me go a bit overboard with it. That's where my mother comes in handy. She encouraged me to focus on narrowing in on the types of people who could really help me get the break I was seeking.

The fundamental life principles that my parents instilled in me contributed toward my persistence. However, since I was an only child, I developed the syndrome of thinking the world revolves around me and that I am special. In Hollywood, it's quite the opposite. Every writer thinks they have the best script. Every actor thinks they are deserving of a leading film role. My mother often reminds me there will always be someone better— smarter, prettier and more talented. She suggests focusing on being the best you were called to be in this lifetime. My mother's realness is sometimes annoying. Whenever I talk about my dreams and my destiny, she gives me the reality check I need.

"Nothing happens without hard work, planning, execution, and faith," she'd say.

"But if you are destined to be a top surgeon, don't you think it will happen in God's timing?" I'd ask.

"If you don't apply to go to medical school, spend countless hours studying, and do your residency, you will miss out on your destiny," she'd declare.

In addition to my A-list parents, there is a group of other mentors who impacted my life at various stages of my career. I met most of my mentors by reaching out to them for an information meeting (IM). I found IMs are the best way to go about finding a mentor. I always encourage interns within my non-profit and BiH members to try and set-up meetings as often as they can with industry pros. As someone once explained to me, an informational meeting is with someone you respect or admire. Establishing a mentor is great because they can provide advice and help you make wise career decisions. Informational meetings can also be an opportunity to learn about a successful person's journey. Meetings with celebrities or prominent industry professionals are particularly useful because they give you an inside perspective into their showbiz journey. While the trade magazines may report that a person's first screenplay sold for $10M, the article doesn't say he had written five scripts prior, and had been trying to sell the script that sold for 15 years.

Through every informational meeting I had, I learned something new. Sometimes the meetings were extremely valuable. Other times, I may have just received a small piece of advice that triggered a new idea or thought that ultimately helped my career in some way.

The list below includes industry professionals whom I met through an informational meeting. Many of these people I met more than once or maintained a relationship with them after the initial meeting. The asterisks represent those who introduced me to somebody else on the list. An executive at Paramount recommended every time I meet a helpful mentor, ask them to introduce me to someone else in their circle. The list below is partial, but I wanted to share it to give an idea of the level of professionals I was able to secure meetings with within a two-year period. If I did it, anyone with the desire can too!

Informational Meetings
Agent, Agency West
Vice President of Development & Acquisitions, BET
Director, Bill Cosby Writing Program
Director of CAA Foundation, CAA
Senior Vice President of Diversity, CBS
Producer, ("Collateral", "Save The Last Dance") *
Attorney, Del, Shaw, Moonves, Tanaka, Finkelstein & Lezcano
Vice President of Feature Animation Production, Disney
Vice President of Diversity, Disney Writing Program
Director of Human Resources & Diversity, Dreamworks *
Creative Director, Edmonds Entertainment
Senior Vice President of Home Entertainment,
Entertainment Studios
Producer, MTV Films ("Fighting Temptations")
Writer, ("Fighting Temptation")
Producer/Manager, The Firm
Senior Vice President of Development, First Move
Television Production
Vice President of Current Programming, Fox
Vice President of Members Services, Grammys*

Staff Writer/Co-Producer, Sitcom "Half & Half"
Founder, Hollywood Black Resource Center
Agent, ICM
Creative Executive, MGM
Vice President of Home Entertainment, MGM
Vice President of International Television Distribution, MGM *
Writer, Sitcom "My Wife & Kids" *
Vice President of Production & Development, NBC
Vice President of Programming & Development, NBC
Executive Vice President of Diversity, NBC
Marketing Manager, New Line Cinema
Vice President of Development, New Line Cinema
Director of Writer's Fellowship, Nickelodeon
Producer/Director of Creative Affairs, Paramount
Senior Vice President of Comedy Development, Paramount
Vice President of Development, Paramount
Director of Acquisitions, Showtime Networks *
Senior Vice President of Movies & Miniseries, Sony
Pictures Television
Director of Worldwide Recruitment, Time Warner
Vice President of Development & Acquisitions,
Urban Entertainment
Vice President of Productions & Acquisitions, Warner
Independent Pictures
Senior Vice President of Development, Warner Bros. Television
Director of Current Programming, Warner Bros. Television
Director of Recruitment, Warner Bros. Television*
Agent, William Morris Endeavor

Family
What I love most about my parents is they emphasized the value
of having a balanced life. They also led me to meet and marry
my college sweetheart. They taught me a lot of strategic dating
lessons on how men think, and that helped me take Arthur off
the market. Also, although my parent's marriage of 15 years
didn't last forever, they still gave me the confidence to believe
it can and will work for me if I believe and do what it takes to
make it happen.

My husband Arthur and I have known each other for
14 years and have been married for 7 of them. We met at the

deli-counter on the engineering campus at the University of Michigan. Unlike some couples, we actually agree on how we met. He was working in the cafeteria behind the cold cut counter. He was in charge of making the sandwich I selected.

As I approached the counter, I thought to myself, "Wow, he's handsome!"

I was next in line and before giving my order I asked, "What's your name?"

He stood there for about 5 seconds completely silent.

I waved my hand and said louder, "Hello! What's your name?"

He just looked at me again like he was star struck.

Finally, he spattered out, "Arthur."

"Hi Arthur. It's nice to meet you. I'm Angela," I replied.

We smiled at each other. Not sure what sandwich he made for me, but after that day he spoke to me with such confidence, unlike our first encounter. He often reminded me that he was the cafeteria guy. I knew exactly who he was from that day forward ... my husband! Well, I didn't know it definitely, but my always-right mother did. After Arthur and I became friends, we had a small little falling out. I called my mother and told her that I was worried this guy wouldn't speak to me again because I had made a rude comment to him.

My mother said, "It doesn't sound serious. Why are you obsessing over it?"

"What do you mean?" I replied.

"Oh my goodness ..." she said.

"What?" I asked sincerely.

"This is the man you are going to marry," she declared.

"Mother, you are ridiculous. I don't like the guy like that at all. He's just my friend."

"Friend today, husband tomorrow," she said.

"Oh my gosh, mother you are annoying and wrong," I said as I hung up the phone.

I don't know whether it's that my mother is actually always right or when she puts thoughts into my mind about a certain subject, I somehow let it happen. I'm still unclear to this day whether she uses some form of reverse psychology on me or if she's psychic!

Sure enough, several years later, Arthur became my

very best friend, and then the love of my life. It wasn't an easy road for us to get together. We have definitely had our share of relationship roller coasters, which has made us grow closer in liking and in love. I am eternally grateful for his friendship and support throughout my career. He's been to every Hollywood event I've asked him to attend and always without complaining. He's amazing. I am also truly fascinated by the best gifts he gave me: our 2-year-old son Alexander and new daughter Alyssa. Our children are so precious and definitely make living worthwhile and exciting. Creating a family legacy is an opportunity to explore life all over again.

Friends

Another individual who has been instrumental in my growth as a person is my best friend Sarah-Elizabeth, a beauty queen who competed in Donald Trump's Miss USA pageant. She is such a jewel. We also met at the University of Michigan as college roommates. Over the past 16 years, we developed a truly special friendship. We used to say we love each other like sisters. Until one day, we decided to officially say we are sisters. She has always inspired me to achieve greatness because of her own life and existence. Originally from Atlanta, her late father was a minister and a state senator in Georgia. You can imagine the type of life one lives when a parent is involved in politics and ministry, particularly in a close knit city like Atlanta. Then and today, some of the most prominent African Americans reside there. They have made an influential mark on our society. From Martin Luther King to his good friend Andrew Young, who Sarah knows and has met a few times because of her prominent connection to her beloved Atlanta community.

When I moved to Hollywood, Sarah was extremely supportive. She has always encouraged me to pursue my dreams. She has also been a creative influence and amazing brainstormer throughout my career as I transitioned to different jobs, from being a writer to a talent agent to a casting director, and while developing the non-profit organization, Breaking into Hollywood. Sarah has been with me through it all. Whether or not I was achieving the type of success I wanted, she encouraged me to feel proud of living my dream. I am grateful for Sarah's friendship and for the candid advice she has given me through the years. Destined for greatness—she is indeed!

Another superstar whom it is an honor to have on my A-list is actress Mary Nicole. Since she too has been through the trenches in Hollywood, she has been a remarkable support system. She is the friend who always makes you cry from laughter. No matter the situation, she finds the hilariousness of it. Mary and I met during an interview for talent scout positions. We both got the job. Not really knowing what we were getting into, we decided to partner up with each other. We had to go around Los Angeles finding kids in malls, parks, festivals, or wherever. The pitch was to tell parents how adorable their children were, and then invite them to come and audition. We let them know that if their child was selected, they could make money acting in film/TV shows. At the time, we thought it was 100% legitimate. We simply got paid $50 for every child that showed up for the 'audition'. Bringing in 10 kids, meant $500 for the week plus bonuses. The job's flexibility was incredible; you created your own schedule and determined your scouting locations. We scouted for cute kids whenever and wherever we wanted. We were both pretty good at it, but it was definitely harder than we thought.

Our dream job ended when we unknowingly approached a parent whom we didn't know we had previously met. The mother told us to get away from her and her child because we were scam artists. We couldn't believe what she was saying to us. We innocently pried for more information and got to the bottom of why she was saying such awful things. She explained we had selected her little girl and that she took her to the audition. Then, she said they were asked to pay almost $1,000 to set their child up in the industry as an actress. Huge red flag!

Mary and I weren't really sure how a child breaks into the business. We figured it was probably just like an adult would, and they shouldn't have to pay anything, except for maybe some basic headshots, which should not cost that much (but could depending on the photographer). When we inquired to our boss, he explained more about the company. They offered classes, photos and a bunch of things for the kids' parents to pay for in order to get their kid started in acting, with the hopes of them being able to audition for roles or participate in background roles for Disney shows. It was not legally a scam because they offered products and services for the fee and they didn't make any false promises the child would become a star. Even still, it was not a business I wanted to be affiliated with because I knew in Hollywood, your reputation is everything. Mary and I both had a positive reputation to uphold. We decided to quit at the same time, and laugh about it now. That was one of our many crazy experiences in Hollywood.

I am thankful to have Mary on my A-list also because she is the type of person who really cares for the well-being of her friends. After I had my first baby, Mary continued to be very supportive, doing whatever she could to make my transition into motherhood okay. I love Mary for her delightful sense of humor and her kindred spirit. I hope she becomes one of the great actresses/comediennes of our generation.

TWeLVe

Sleepless Nights in Los Angeles

After living in L.A. for about four years, I came to a point where I felt I had pursued my writing career to the fullest and still had not yet achieved the success I wanted. I knew hundreds of executives. I was affiliated with professional writing organizations. I had developed several writing mentors, as well as other industry mentors. I also made sure to maintain a well-rounded career, focused on nurturing my relationship with my husband and my family. I worked out and ate fairly healthily. I attended church as well as donated my money and time to their various youth programs. I even mentored youth who were aspiring to become writers and actors. Overall, I thought I had put my best foot forward with all I had control over to try to achieve success in the industry.

It was during this year when I really valued my mother and the advice she had given me over the years about thinking positively and never quitting. I felt like there were permanent closed doors preventing me from achieving my goals, or a huge mountain in my way. My mother said once you have tried to go around the mountain, and over the mountain, but still cannot seem to reach the other side, there's only one thing left to do—use dynamite to blow it up!

What she meant was when you are going after a goal or dream that is difficult to achieve, you can't let anything stop you. As I like to say, you have to go after your dream with all the ICE you can find ... Integrity, Creativity and Enthusiasm!

To deal with the no's, you have to remember it may take a 100 no's before you get a yes. But often, all you need is one yes to get you in the game or keep you there depending on where you are in your career. Dealing with rejection as an actor is difficult because actors are the actual product. It can also be challenging for a writer or other professionals because the product they create is an extension of their selves. The best way to deal with depression as it relates to you career is to learn how to create breakthrough success even in the worse situations.

I had several sleepless nights living in Los Angeles when I felt anxious, confused and/or depressed. Ironically, those nights were often the times when I received the best ideas for a project or ways to go about accomplishing a goal. One of the weekends that changed the course of my life for the better was when my husband went to St. Louis for a few days to celebrate with his family. His sister was graduating from graduate school; she had received her doctorate in physical therapy and became the first doctor in the family. I have always been impressed with the upbringing of my husband's family. Neither of Arthur's parents finished college, yet they managed to raise three children who successfully graduated from prominent universities, including Harvard, MIT and the University of Michigan.

The weekend Arthur was away, I started pondering my life and questioning my reasons for moving to L.A. Basically, I was second-guessing myself. Then, I made a phone call to my mother that changed my life.

"What's wrong, Angie?" she asked.

"Nothing's wrong. I'm just calling to say hi," I said.

"I can hear it in your voice. Something is wrong. What's wrong? How's Arthur doing?" she asked.

"He went to St. Louis for his sister's graduation," I said.

"Oh, you're lonely. You're calling me because you miss him," she said jokingly.

"No, mother. I miss you. I was just calling to say hi," I said.

"Angela, what's wrong?" she inquired again.

"Well, I was just thinking about my life ... my career. And I'm not happy with it," I said.

"What's wrong with it?" she asked.

"Well, I moved out here with a plan. And I've done all I could and I still haven't achieved the kind of success I would like with my entertainment career," I explained.

"Did you pray about it?" she asked.

"Yes, but I still don't feel better. I know God is in control, but He also gives us freewill to make decisions and to do the things we need to do in order to accomplish His plan, which hopefully is aligned with our personal goals, but ..." I said.

"But, what?" she asked.

"Well, I just don't have the energy any more to keep pursuing my writing career. And maybe it's not going to happen for me because I've done all I could," I said.

"You could not have possibly done everything," she said.

"Oh, but I have," I said firmly.

"Are you giving back?" she asked.

"Yes, I mentor girls at my church. I'm involved in various charitable activities to help others," I said.

"But what are you doing to give back specifically in the area you want to be successful in?" she asked.

"Nothing really, I guess," I mumbled.

"Well, there you go. You need to find a way to convey all the knowledge you know to others who are up and coming in the industry," she said.

At first the idea seemed pretty ridiculous. Then, after I began to brainstorm it further, I came up with a vision for a non-profit organization that could help people break into Hollywood. I researched other entertainment organizations. I couldn't find one that focused on all the areas of entertainment. Most focused on either actors, writers, producers or directors, respectively, or some combination of those. I wanted to create an organization that would also help aspiring music artists, wardrobe stylists, agents, casting director, entertainment attorneys and managers. I visualized in my mind an organization that helped both creative and business professionals pursue their entertainment careers by providing them with advice, resources and mentors through event speakers. I started thinking of what the organization could be called and instantly, "Breaking into Hollywood" came to mind.

I Googled the name to see if there was an existing organization with that same name. Then I researched the domain to see if *www.breakingintohollywood.org* was available. It was indeed available, and it had never been used before. I kind of thought that was odd because it seemed like such a popular phrase. I told my mom about the vision I had created based on her advice. She loved the idea and was extremely supportive of it. She said the reason the name had never been used was because God was waiting for me to use it. She used to always tell me when God has something for you, no one can take it away. I agree wholeheartedly, but sometimes it's difficult to remember to embrace that concept when you feel things aren't going your way.

On Sunday, when my husband came home, I said, "Guess what?!"

Excited, he replied, "What?"

"I started a business," I said.

He smirked. Then, with a bit of curiosity and hesitation he asked, "Okay ... what kind of business?"

"A non-profit!" I exclaimed.

"A non-profit?" he asked with disappointment.

"Yes, a non-profit organization that will serve the Los Angeles creative community," I explained.

"Why does it have to be not for profit? You have not had a job in almost two years, and you need to be making money!" he exclaimed.

I explained to him that just because it was not for profit didn't mean there wasn't an opportunity for me to work for the organization in the future and have a salary or even receive a stipend until getting to that point. That was a selling point for him. After I explained the purpose of the organization in depth, Arthur was on board! As usual, my husband was extremely supportive of my new endeavor. He is a very kind-hearted person, but he also has a business-oriented mind. When I took the two years off work to write screenplays, Arthur considered that an investment for our future. Similarly, he saw BiH as an investment. While it was created to serve the creative community at large, I would benefit as well.

The very first event for Breaking into Hollywood was held on June 4, 2005. We advertised it on Craigslist and to my various contacts. We had about eight attendees. It was held at the circular hotel off the 405 freeway in Los Angeles, which was then a Holiday Inn hotel (now called Hotel Angelino). At the workshop, I covered a variety of topics that I'll discuss in detail within this chapter. I had my two friends Michelle (from MGM) and Maria (from the reality TV show) speak briefly as well.

The event began with me giving the opening remarks and an icebreaker. I always find icebreakers are a great way to start an event, particularly one related to Hollywood because so much of breaking into Hollywood is about networking. You never know who the person you are sitting next to will become in the next 10 years. I spoke briefly about why I started the organization. Then, I addressed how I felt like I had hit rock bottom with my writing career, but the rock I had fallen on was God's vision for my life and that's how Breaking into Hollywood was born. In the opening session, I explained how I met my first mentor. I'd like to share this story with you because it has a few layers that may pique your interest or motivate you to take action.

When I was working at Spotlight Health, the entertainment public relation firm I mentioned previously, a new employee named Samantha was hired as the marketing director. She was down-to-earth and candid. We discovered that we shared a common goal of becoming a professional scriptwriter. Samantha wanted to write for soap operas. Two days after she was hired, she informed me about her decision to quit. Samantha had received a job offer to work at ICM in the agency's mailroom. We both knew that meant a huge salary reduction from her current position, about $75K to $25K. Quitting a good paying job seemed ludicrous. I mean, at least earn some decent money for a few weeks at the PR firm, and then go be poor working in an agency's mailroom. Samantha explained this was part of her master plan. By working at a prominent agency, she believed she would gain industry insight and have much more access than she had now. She wanted to use the job to get to know who the industry power players were and establish how to develop relationships with them.

Although the salary to work in the mailroom is mediocre, it is still difficult to land such a job at a top agency. I have heard stories of attorneys who have applied to work in the mailroom and were denied. Not because they were overqualified, more so because the agency didn't feel they had the passion and drive to make it in such a fast-paced, cut-throat environment. That's what I was told by a hiring manager at a top agency.

Samantha said she got the job by getting a referral through her alumni network at Northwestern University. She strongly encouraged me to look into my own alumni network. I just kind of blew off her suggestion because I didn't see how contacting my alumni network could be beneficial at all, especially since I had majored in engineering. I didn't have any ties to the communications department at Michigan. Regardless, she was still very persistent in telling me to do so. I still disregarded her advice and just took it as a grain of salt. She and I didn't keep in touch because at the time, I didn't really understand the value of networking and maintaining relationships. I was more focused on knowledge and meeting only specific people who I thought could directly help my career. If I couldn't figure out how someone could be useful in helping me achieve my goals, I would pretty much disregard them, just like I did her.

Less than a year later, I was reading *Creative Screenwriting* magazine. There was a section that featured a success story, and the picture of a woman caught my eye. Sure enough, it was Samantha. The article talked about how she had landed a job as a writer for a soap opera. She attributed her success to her alumni network. I read the article in awe. The next day, I researched online and reached out to my alumni network. I found out University of Michigan had several alumni living in Los Angeles who were working in the entertainment industry. The school's alumni center provided me with an e-mail list of about 100 people. It was during this time I was tired of working at Spotlight Health, and like Samantha, I wanted a change. I was ready to achieve my goal of becoming a screenwriter. I sent a brief mass e-mail Bcc-ing everyone, stating who I was, where I was from, and my career goals. I asked if anyone would be willing to meet with me to offer some advice.

Believe it or not, out of the 100 people I e-mailed, I only received a reply from one person. Although the others didn't respond, it was like receiving 99 "No, I cannot help you" replies. But remember, all you need is one yes. The woman who responded to my e-mail, her name was also Angela. Later, I found out her name was Angela Marie, just like mine. She told me that was the reason for her wanting to meet with me. Who would have known something that simple would trigger someone to meet with me? Anyhow, she responded that day. We scheduled a brief meeting for the following week. I was excited because her e-mail footer showed her title as a vice president at MGM.

When I arrived at her office, I buzzed in and said my name. She actually came out to the floor's lobby area and greeted me. To my surprise, she was African American, and to her surprise, I was African American.

She asked, "Angela?" while reaching out her hand out to shake mine. "Wow, I didn't know you were black. I've never met another Angela Marie who was black."

We bonded over several moments of laughter. It was pretty funny to us because we were both expecting the other person to be white. Angela took me under her wings and said she would introduce me to everyone she knew. She told me the way I was going to break into Hollywood was by meeting as many people as possible. She also told me to never quit, no matter how difficult my journey. She actually made me promise right there in her office to not quit and to promise to meet as many people as possible, and so I did. She gave me the contact information for several other prominent industry execs. She said they would definitely meet with me once I told them she referred me.

One of Angela's best friends, Karla, was a television writer for ABC's "My Wife and Kids." She was very helpful also and gave me advice about how to get ahead as a woman, particularly a black woman. We met at Roscoe's House of Chicken n' Waffles. There, I was introduced to L.A.'s popular egg whites. Karla ordered a waffle with egg whites and fried chicken. I ordered what she ordered. Since then, pretty much all I eat is scrambled egg whites, especially after finding out they are less fattening and healthier than eating regular scrambled eggs.

Meeting Angela was a blessing I will never forget. It was her advice, wisdom, and encouragement that allowed me to meet over 100 prominent industry professionals who met with me one-on-one at their offices or for dinner, lunch, or coffee. Unfortunately, I have lost contact with Angela because I believe she moved overseas, and I wasn't the best at keeping up with people then, especially when things were busy for me. I am sure she is doing well, and I hope we will connect again someday. She knows I am thankful because I always told her whenever she would take me to lunch. I always expressed my gratitude for her taking such a liking to me and mentoring me.

At the Breaking into Hollywood new members' workshop, I shared that story. Many people were then encouraged to reach out to their alumni network or, at the very least, pay more attention to advice that people gave them instead of disregarding it upfront. After the brief story, I addressed the critical questions many people have when first moving to L.A., as well as those who may have already been here for some time but needed a jumpstart with a new thought or perspective on breaking into Hollywood. The morning's first topics were:

How do I get a job in the entertainment industry?
How can I maximize my networking potential?
How do I develop my writing or acting craft with limited $$$?

Getting a job in the entertainment industry. We talked about the UTA job list, which at the time was a hot commodity. It was a list compiled of various industry jobs you could only get if someone e-mailed it to you. I was receiving the e-mail list from different mentors. As a member benefit to joining BiH, we would e-mail the list to our members. We also talked about Workplace Hollywood (*www.workplacehollywood.org*), which is one of Hollywood's best kept secrets. It's a non-profit organization that specializes in job placement, similar to an employment agency, but slightly different. They have a job development division that helps people perfect their resumes and helps them secure mentorships and internships. They also hold various job events to help people connect with entertainment industry human resource professionals.

Maximizing networking potential. In order to meet the most relevant people for your career, joining professional organizations like BiH is critical. There is a list of BiH's recommended industry organizations one should join for a specific craft, as well as useful industry resources listed in the appendix of this book.

The other way to network is through informational

meetings (IMs). During the orientation, we discussed what to say in an IM request letter and also what to discuss during the meeting. The purpose of such a meeting isn't necessarily to get someone to read your script or to audition you for a role. It is more to obtain their advice and to develop an initial relationship with the person with the hopes of it furthering into a mentorship. There is a myth that only college students obtain IMs. Anyone can secure such a meeting, but they must be strategic in their approach. There are a few books specifically on this topic, as well as articles. I would encourage all those interested in learning more about informational meetings to research the topic online.

Developing a craft with limited funds. It can be expensive to continuously attend networking events, conferences and expos. It can also be equally or more expensive to invest in subscriptions to industry publications, books, or other resources. One of the ways I encourage BiH members to develop their writing, acting or singing craft is to research the various speakers that attend local events and contact them directly via mail or e-mail to schedule an IM. Generally, the speakers who are out speaking at these various industry functions are open to giving information and advice. These are the people who typically make good mentors. If you can't afford to attend every festival and conference in town, research the invited speakers. Then, a few weeks after the event has passed, contact them directly to see if they will meet with you briefly in person. Also, you can request a short phone meeting as an alternative to an in-person meeting. Any amount of time with an established professional can be valuable. One piece of advice can trigger great ideas.

      As for the different industry publications, instead of buying a subscription to *Variety*, *Hollywood Reporter* or *Back Stage*, I visited local bookstores that had coffee shops inside. I would take several magazines and skim them for any valuable information. For those that didn't have coffee shops, I would simply cop a squat on the floor and skim away. Nowadays, many bookstores put certain publications behind their registers because they don't want people doing this very thing. There are some bookstores particularly those in the suburbs or outskirts of

Los Angeles, that still leave the industry pubs with the regular magazines. To have access to these costly publications, you can also consider talking several other industry friends into splitting a subscription or membership with you. This also could work for an IMDb pro account, which is great for valuable research. Also, the Learning Annex offers fairly cheap prices on classes on specific topics like how to get cast, how to get an agent, how to sell a script, how to get a music deal, etc. Those can be useful as well, but again I encourage people who cannot afford to attend these seminars to attempt to contact the speaker after the event has passed.

After answering the popular three questions just addressed, I continued on with our agenda for the "How to Jumpstart Your Career" workshop.

It's a Numbers Game. It is often said breaking into Hollywood is like winning the lotto. They say it's a numbers game because like with anything, there are statistics associated with the success rate of those who are actually making it to A-list status in the industry. In our new members' orientation, we provided three tips to help increase one's chances of becoming a success story.

1) *Look at the Whole Picture.* If you don't look at the whole picture you might miss out on your blessings. It is important to stay focused, but not so focused you disregard opportunities. There is a number's game I have shown to hundreds of new members, and not one single person ever got it correct. First, I asked everyone to gather around. I explained that I am going to throw down the markers and pens in my hand onto this table (or sometimes I used the floor), and that I wanted them tell me how many numbers they saw.

"Does everyone understand?" I would ask.

Everyone always nodded in agreement.

I then took my handful of writing utensils and threw them down. I would ask everyone what number they saw. They would ask me what I meant.

"Do you mean how many pens you threw down, or do you mean what shape the pens made as they lay scattered?" some might ask.

"All I can say is, what number do you see?" I repeated.

After people shouted out random numbers, I would confidently say the number I saw. I would do this for at least five or six times. Every time, no one, I mean not one single person, ever got this right. Finally, I would let everyone in on the game. I would show them that every time I threw down the pens, I was changing the number of fingers on my hands, which was always displayed very obviously on the table or ground directly next to the pens. But even still, no one ever noticed I was changing my fingers. No one. Isn't that interesting? The fact that I could show over 100 different types of people that game and no one would guess it right!

The purpose of the game was to express the idea that breaking into Hollywood doesn't have to be a number's game if you learn to look at the whole picture. If you are so focused on the task at hand or your specific goal, you will without a doubt miss obvious opportunities that may be presented to you or great ideas that may come your way to guide you to a particular path on your dream journey.

2) *Can't be Afraid to Ask.* It is said you have not because you ask not. It's important to always ask for that job or role or writing gig. My father used to say the difference between you getting a job and not getting a job might be simply that you didn't ask for it, or the opposite—you were the only one to actually ask for it, displaying you had more of a sincere interest than others applying.

3) *Be Resourceful.* In the entertainment industry, people always want to take, take, take. People will try to take your time, connections or resources, and to some extent that is okay. It is important to be resourceful not just about your specific craft within the industry, but other crafts as well. Helping a friend or associate achieve their goals can be rewarding. An actress told me every time she had an audition, she told friends who were her type about the audition and provided them with all of the details. She encouraged them to try and 'crash' the audition with the hopes of being able to slip in an audition and actually be considered for the role. Even though they may not have been given the audition information because they may not have had an agent representing them to send them out, or whatever the reason, she always helped her friends. I asked her if she was afraid a friend might get a role she was supposed

to have, or could have had, if she had not informed her friend. She said whatever is for her is for her and no one can take that away. That's a substantive principle to live by while in pursuit of difficult goals.

The next part of the new members' orientation consisted of addressing these following questions:

Do I need an agent or manager?
How do I find good representation?
How do I get a studio or agency to read my script?

Having an agent or manager. Whether or not it is necessary to have an agent while pursuing a music, acting, writing, or even a directing career often comes into question at various events and panel discussions. The answer to do you need an agent or manager, is NO!

Having an agent or manager can indeed be helpful, but it is not mandatory, particularly if you are in the aspiring stages. An agent only makes 10% of the talent's money. The talent makes the other 90%. Therefore, the talent should be responsible for 90% of their career, and their representation only 10%.

The minute some actors get an agent, they sit back and relax, waiting for the phone to ring with auditions. That may work for some agents, but many agents prefer a client who is socializing, networking and professionally hustling for their next gig. In our new members' orientation, we explain it like this: If an agent gets their actor client an audition or their writer client a meeting with a development exec, and if that talent knows other people in the room through networking they had previously done, that can help close the deal or land them the gig. In this town, there are thousands of talented professionals. Often talent is not always hired based on talent, but on who they know or who knows them.

Until you have an agent or manager, be your own! Learn everything you can about the business side of the industry and develop a great pitch for yourself. If an actor or writer finds a way to book their own gigs, when a good agent or manager takes them on, they will soar.

At the end of the day, the ball is always in your court at all times. You cannot rely on an agent or manager or anyone to help you take your career to the next level. As an actor, writer or almost any industry professional, you are the CEO of your company. It is up to you to determine the plan of action and begin to execute it. As your company (you/your brand) grows and becomes somewhat of a branded product, then it is time for you to focus on getting more players on your team. However, there is really not a reason to hire an agent or manager to work for you when you don't have a clear sense of direction for your goals.

Finding good representation. When talent thinks of representation they often think of an agent or manager. Representation also includes an attorney, publicist, accountant, friends, and even mentors. When you think of finding good representation, think of finding a team of people that can best represent you, your talents, and your goals.

    One of the best ways agents and managers tend to accept new clients is through referrals. That can sometimes seem like another industry catch 22. If you just moved to Los Angeles, you likely won't have any good contacts or may not know anyone who can give you a referral. If that is the case, you aren't quite ready for representation anyway. Your focus should be to network like crazy. You do this by attending events through professional organizations like Breaking into Hollywood, Scriptwriters Network, Film Independent, Women in Film, Changing Images in America, Organization of Black Screenwriters, National Association of Latino Independent Producers, Coalition of Asian Pacifics in Entertainment, National Academy of Recording Arts & Sciences, Los Angeles Women in Music, etc. (See the Appendix.)

    You can also increase your network through informational meetings or by attending social events and certain parties at night clubs, particularly when it is in conjunction with an industry party such as the launching of a new product or show. We always encourage people who attend our BiH events to use BiH as a referral because the attendees have indeed met the speaker. Almost all of the time, our speakers will tell you that is referral enough. Generally, an agent is not trying to play hardball with only accepting referrals, nor is a manager trying to be the tough gal or guy—it's simply about time management.

In any given week, my former agency received 100+ headshots of actors submitting for representation. We had assistants and interns who went through every single photo and put them into No, Yes and Maybe bins. At the agents' leisure, we would browse the bins when there was down time, and we may decide to call in one person per month. However, if any submission came with a letter mentioning they were referred by someone or met us somewhere, the interns would be instructed to automatically put them into the Yes bin to be contacted for a meeting. Even the Yes pile actors weren't always contacted because after looking at the picture, we may have decided the actor is too similar to an existing client or there isn't a lot of work for their type based on the daily casting breakdowns. But at least that referral got them into the Yes pile, which helped to make their submission less of a numbers game.

Getting a studio or agency to read your script. Many writers think you must absolutely have a manager, agent or an attorney to get your script read by a prominent agency, studio or production company. But all you really need is confidence. How do you get them to read your material without representation? You simply ask!

One way to get a studio to read your script is to develop a relationship with a mentor, and then ask them if they can send your script to their coverage department. They provide coverage within agencies, production companies and studios. If the coverage on your project truly stands out, your mentor, or maybe the reader of the coverage, may try to get your script into the right person's hands, which can lead to the next step with the company buying your script or getting it produced.

One of my studio executive mentors offered to have my script covered within her company. Even though the script wasn't right for the network, having professional coverage of my script was useful. When I first reviewed the coverage, it was awful. Not the coverage, but the things said about my script were not the most positive. It helped me realize I needed to do more rewriting. The next time I received coverage on that same script from another studio, the coverage on the story was much better.

As BiH grew into a more established organization, I, as the founder, grew into a more established industry professional.

A story I often shared during our new members' orientation is one that I hope inspires and encourages writers to be confident in their material and politely, yet tenaciously, ask that it be read. By expressing a voice that demands to be heard, people will listen and will give you a chance because no one wants to pass up on the next best thing.

I was reading the *Hollywood Reporter* just after Tyler Perry's first movie at Lions Gate arrived in theaters, making millions and surpassing the studio's expectations. The article quoted several Lions Gate executives on a variety of topics. One of the executives' quotes mentioned they were seeking similar scripts, but written by women of color. I figured I am a black woman and I have a similar script. So, I went on to Google and searched for the e-mail address domain of Lions Gate's e-mails. Typically, you can find the e-mail address of anyone at a company. Once you know one person's e-mail, you can figure out another person's e-mail as long as you have their first and last name. The public relations department of most studios always have a point of contact in its PR/marketing department who provides a person's e-mail at the end of a press release. Utilize that to your advantage. I sure did.

Once I figured out the e-mail format for the company, I sent individual e-mails to the four or five people who had been quoted in the article. I e-mailed them an unsolicited query e-mail and pitched myself as an up-and-coming screenwriter. I included my writing background and the information on the specific screenplay I wanted them to consider. Within just a few hours, I received a response from one of the executives telling me to e-mail them the script and to fill out the attached release form they provided.

Without an agent, manager or attorney, I was able to submit my script to Lions Gate. I had an attorney friend of mine review the release agreement, and he said it was a terribly biased agreement. By sending my script, I couldn't sue them if they came out with a similar movie. From that standpoint, it may have been better to have an agent or manager send it, but the fact is I didn't have one. So there wasn't really a choice to be made. I did what I set out to do, which was to get my script to Lions Gate. I faxed back the release form and e-mailed my script to the executive.

The next day, she got back to me and said although she felt I was a good writer with a distinct voice, the script wasn't what they were looking for at the time. First off, I could not believe she had read the script so fast. I e-mailed her back and thanked her for reading it, but I also inquired about specifically what type of script they were looking to produce. She said they were looking for a movie along the lines of "Waiting to Exhale" for a black female audience. Although my script had some components of that film, it certainly wasn't a chick flick like "Waiting to Exhale."

Anyhow, I asked the executive if she would be willing to meet with me because I would love to pick her brain to gain more knowledge about how the studio system works and learn more about how Tyler Perry's project was produced there. She agreed, and we met a few weeks later at MTV's cafeteria for lunch, which was next to Lions Gate. We met for about an hour and a half. She was very informative and gave me insider information of how the studio operates, how projects are greenlighted, how Tyler's project was selected to be produced there, and much more! It was an eye-opening meeting. Although I didn't sell my script, I did achieve my goal, which was to have my script read at a studio without having an agent or manager. I kept in touch with that executive as she moved on to become a vice president at another production company, but then I lost touch with her. As I said, maintaining relationships can be a challenge, especially if you have lots of contacts you are developing at the same time.

It is indeed beneficial to be selective with the mentors you develop and the relationships you decide to build. If you create a plan for your relationships, you won't lose touch with people simply because you have forgotten about them since you are focused on the next new industry contact.

Following the second set of questions of the new members' orientation, we talked to members about the importance of creating a plan of action. A written plan of action can be more useful than just trying to remember goals in your head. A written plan allows you to hold yourself accountable for achieving your goals. Next, we had an open Q&A session where members addressed their specific questions, concerns or needs. Finally, we had closing remarks and concluded the session with my favorite inspirational poem entitled, "Don't Quit!" (See Chapter 16.)

Overall, Breaking into Hollywood's first event turned out to be very productive and a great success. I received e-mails from all those who had attended saying it was one of the best events they had ever attended in L.A. As a federally recognized 501(c)(3) non-profit organization, Breaking into Hollywood, has been in existence since May 2005. Recently, the organization held its 2nd Annual Industry Job Summit with participating companies such as Warner Bros., Nickelodeon and CBS. There where were over 500 attendees, which is a long way from the first event with eight participants. BiH continues to strive toward achieving its mission of helping creative and business professionals pursue their entertainment careers with integrity, creativity and enthusiasm.

The sleepless nights I had as a result of not being happy with my writing career led to breakthrough success with BiH. Learning to deal with the no's and rejections by creating some form of success, may just lead to your next breakthrough instead of another sleepless night in Los Angeles.

THiRTeeN

Hollywood Chaos

There comes a time in every artist's life where they become frustrated with the industry. They consider taking matters into their own hands and decide to take more control of their career. Similar to the movie *Office Space*, when the disgruntled and mentally abused employees steal the company's money and blow the building down, literally!

This breaking point often arises for a writer, actor or director who can't seem to secure representation. For the actor, maybe they have an agent but aren't getting the auditions they want, so they may decide to put on a one-woman/man show. A producer or director who's been trying to raise money for a feature film may decide to shoot a low-budget short film or produce a play. A writer may decide to have a live reading with actors or produce a web series, or even try to produce their script themselves due to the exhaustion of submitting to agents, managers or production companies. A music artist frustrated with not being able to secure a record deal, may release his own CD and focus on street sales.

This breaking or revolutionary point is the time when artists take on the chaos in Hollywood, trying to create their own opportunities. For some, success is achieved. Unfortunately however, for many, the specific success they were seeking is not achieved. But for all, a learning experience always takes place. The artist receives new and necessary tools for their career toolbox that will ultimately come in handy as they reach and maintain their desired level of success.

My revolutionary moment arrived when I was sitting in the audience for an event being hosted by my organization,

Breaking into Hollywood. It was entitled, "A Night with Creative Stars," which was a panel of producers and actors. Not the most famous producers, but indeed ones who were making a living from producing. And the actors although not famous, were established with a strong list of IMDb credits. It was a productive event because the panelists had achieved a level of success that many of the audience members were striving to achieve. For the audience to hear from these professionals was inspiring because they felt like success in Hollywood was obtainable.

During the panel, I was thinking about how I had met each of the panelists. As for one of the actors on the panel, my mother and I first saw Mykel in a play by David E. Talbert, "Love on Lay-a-Way," at the Wilton Theater in Los Angeles. It was an entertaining play. At the end, they introduced the director and the cast. When the announcer introduced one of the characters, Kalif, the women in the theater went crazy, shouting and screaming. My mother and I were wondering if the man was famous. We didn't recognize him as a famous actor, but we were sitting pretty far back, so we couldn't really see his face. They announced he had just won the cable reality TV show competition, "I Wanna Be A Soapstar." I wasn't into reality TV, so I wasn't familiar with the show. But obviously, the thousands of people in the theater definitely knew who he was, especially the screaming women.

When we were leaving the play, there was this woman outside passing out flyers (who later I found out was his wife). She gave a flyer to my mother.

I glanced at it and said to myself, "He looks a lot like how I had envisioned one of the characters in my screenplay."

Before I started writing my script, *Hollywood Chaos*, I cut out pictures from magazines of what I thought the characters looked like. That way, I could visualize them as I wrote their lines.

As my mom and I walked to our car from the play, I asked my mother, "Doesn't he look a lot like the abusive husband character from my screenplay?"

Smiling, my mother said, "You should hold on to the flyer. Maybe one day he can play the role."

I chuckled, and we went on about our lives. Fast forward two years later, and I was cleaning out my keepsake box. I saw his postcard and thought he would make a good speaker for an upcoming BiH event. Sure enough, I reached out to Mykel through his manager. He agreed to participate as a speaker for free. Since BiH is a non-profit organization, we ask the speakers to donate their time, which enables us to keep the event cost low for the participants, who are often tight on money and without stable jobs. BiH strives to create affordable access for its members and the creative community-at-large.

After the Creative Stars panel, I spoke with Mykel, and I told him how his look reminded me of a character in my script. I said it would be a great role for him to play. He asked to read the script. I explained that it wasn't being produced or anything, and it's just a script I wrote.

He said, "Cool. You can produce it too. I want to read it".

"Okay," I replied. "I will send it to you."

I e-mailed him the script the next day, and he got back to me in a few weeks and said he loved the story and the journey of the character, the one I thought would be intriguing for him to play. He said he wanted the role and told me to focus on finding the money to make the movie because he wants to be in the film. I was wondering to myself why he was saying it like it was so simple. Maybe it was ... I had no clue. I decided since he liked the script, I should get the script to actors who I could see in the roles and see if they would be interested. I thought maybe if I attached talent to the project, somehow I could attract the money through an investor or studio. I then got an idea to cast the whole movie with reality TV stars because many of them were actually actors who resorted to reality TV for fame or saw it as an opportunity rather than a distraction from their TV acting jobs.

I brainstormed the idea with my mother and a few friends, and they liked it. So I moved forward. Since one of my actress friends had done some casting in Atlanta, she agreed to be the casting director. We released the character breakdowns through Breakdown Services, the main casting service for films. Even though we didn't have the money for the film yet, we moved forward on faith. On the casting breakdown, we stated we needed strong actors, but they must have been in some reality TV show as a contestant. Within minutes, we had hundreds of submissions from known reality TV stars to prominent actors who had been on celebrity reality TV shows from channels such as MTV and VH-1. It was really amazing to see all of the submissions and interested actors.

We continued to move forward and scheduled auditions. During the process, I received an e-mail from a very prominent reality TV star from "The Apprentice." We wondered why he would be interested in acting since he was on a business show, unlike the other more fluffy reality shows. His manager who was a good friend of his said his client is an opportunist. So we sent him the script. He read it in a few weeks. He said he loved the script and wanted to help get it made from a producing standpoint. He agreed to fly out to L.A. on his own dime for the auditions and to talk about joining as a producer.

All I could think was, "Wow!"

Two weeks ago, I just had a script. Now, I have auditions scheduled and a potential producer who could work with us to find investors.

At this point, I also started meeting with different directors and sending them the script to see if there was an interest, along with directors of photography (DPs). After just a few weeks, I had established several interested directors one of whom had directed Angela Bassett, another who had directed Ice Cube and another famous TV actor who was transitioning into directing and had just completed his film directorial debut. I couldn't believe these people had read my script and thought it was good enough to direct.

I'll never forget one of my meetings at the Four Seasons hotel in Beverly Hills with a DP who used to be Vice President of Production at Warner Bros. He had my script in hand during the meeting. He said it was truly a movie he wanted to make and a story that needed to be told. I tried to act confident, but I almost wanted to cry with excitement.

I asked him, "Really?"

He said, "Yes Angela, the writing is done very well, and the story is a poignant one that uncovers a message Hollywood hasn't seen yet."

I couldn't believe what I was hearing. A man with years of experience who had worked at a top studio and who then retired to focus on becoming a director of photography, was saying these wonderful things about my screenplay. It was unbelievable to me. He even went into specifics about the script and scenes. It wasn't like he just said generic things that sounded like what I wanted to hear so we would select him as the DP. Then on top of this, I had a crew of about 10 people in various areas of production, including a music supervisor, production assistants, and interns, who were all volunteering their time to focus on making this movie happen. I established this volunteer production crew through an ad posting online with the help of my friend Craig better known as Craigslist—my favorite website of all times.

While producing *Hollywood Chaos*, it was then when I realized although agents, managers and execs are the main gatekeepers to Hollywood, there are plenty side doors. These interested directors and actors wanted to work and make a good movie. They weren't bothered by a lot of the politics that concerns some of the industry insiders. During the first set of auditions which we held at a local dance studio, our producing team had an absolute blast. It was a fun learning experience. We saw tons of reality TV stars, many of who were winners or finalists from shows such as "American Idol," "America's Next Top Model," "Survivor," and "The Apprentice." I remember when the first actor came into the room and auditioned for the role of the basketball player who had to do this robot dance, it was so interesting to see someone do and say what I had written on the page. I also learned some lines didn't seem to work as well when said out loud by the actor. It now made sense why writers and directors have actors perform live stage readings. It's a good tool to use for refining a script.

After the first round of auditions, our team agreed although we had seen a significant amount of talent and could fill some of the roles, we didn't really see anyone who could be the lead character. That was a critical point to the cast. We started brainstorming actors who were not reality TV stars to see if they had an interest. We thought of a host of young female actors and contacted several of them through their agents and managers. All of them pretty much said their clients were not interested and they didn't respond well to the material.

But I was thinking to myself, "How could they have not

responded well to the material in one day?"

I found it hard to believe they had their clients read the script in that one day. Later, we tried a few different tactics through relationships of people that personally knew these actresses to find out if the actors had in fact read the scripts, and that's when we discovered we were right.

The few actors we did connect with had not even heard of the script; their management team served as a block. They only wanted their clients to be attached to fully-financed projects. From their perspective, they don't want producers trying to raise money by dragging their client's name around town. Trying to attach a lead actress to the film with no money was indeed a difficult process. We put the other roles on hold until we found the lead because we knew that was a critical component to getting the movie financed. We moved forward, actively pursuing a famous actress. We went through her management and agent, who said she had the script but would need a few weeks to read.

Then, we had an ironic situation happen when one of our production assistants, Liz, was driving in Westwood and was at a stoplight. Liz said she glanced to her left, and there was Tina-Marie, the actress we wanted for our movie. Liz couldn't believe her eyes. She tried to get her attention by waving. Finally, Tina looked in Liz's direction and rolled down her window to see what Liz was trying to mouth.

Overly excited and quite frantic, our production assistant asked Tina to pull over and she did. Later, we found out Liz came off like a stalker. Tina-Marie gave Liz what we thought was her personal e-mail address. We sent the script and follow-up e-mails. Then, we discovered our production assistant had sent way too many follow-up e-mails. One of the e-mails appeared a bit desperate. Liz told the actress that she wanted to work with her even if she didn't want to work on this movie. It was embarrassing for our team to find out all that had transpired. To say the least, the production assistant apologized, and we knew then she was not one who could work directly with talent because she was too star struck. The actress Tina-Marie, she of course never responded to the e-mails either because she was probably freaked out by the situation, or she may have given us a fake e-mail. Although, the e-mail surely did seem like it could have been her actual account based on the e-mail address, but who knows.

After several months of putting all the pieces together of producing the film, we realized we needed a name producer or at least a respected industry professional to become the executive producer. I pitched the project to one of my close mentors and she agreed to be an executive producer, which meant we could use her name as a pitching tool when trying to get actors attached or investors interested. As we started to attach some name actors, we started to shy away from using the reality TV stars whom we had initially considered from our casting sessions. When we discovered we were able to get name actors involved, we focused on attaching them. There were weeks when things were moving forward with the project and other weeks when the project seemed dead, like we were hamsters in a cage spinning our wheels.

Putting together all the pieces—the cast and the financing, started to feel overwhelming. I remember the day when I had pretty much given up on pursuing the project, I received an interesting phone call that refueled me. I was waiting in line to be an audience member for a new talk show one of my actress friends asked me to attend with her to make a few extra bucks and to see the new show. As we were checking in, I was checking my voice-mail and I had a message from a talent agent who represented an A-list music star. The star was also a rising actress and had starred in one or two hit films. I called her back immediately. Her agent informed me that she was tracking projects for her client. Then, she asked me about the status of *Hollywood Chaos*.

I explained to the agent that we hadn't been able to secure a lead, and we were still seeking the financing, but we had a director in place, along with other names of actors attached. She then told me to give her a call back once the financing was in place, but she said her client is very interested in this role. She hadn't even read the script, so it was kind of odd for her to be very interested, but I understood her point. We exchanged contact information, and I e-mailed her the script later that day. I followed up a few times, but unfortunately, with no financing, we had no lead actress. We never reached the point of actually securing the financing. We came close, but not close enough.

My last time of actively pursuing the project was when we met with Laura, an executive from a newly launched production company that was going to be producing a slate of films. The company was backed by a well-established company and investors. We met at the Peninsula hotel and talked about the project. The executive seemed excited about it, but also seemed more excited about another project I was hoping to also develop down the line. That's probably one lesson I learned is when someone is interested in one project, keep their focus there. Don't start introducing new projects to them because it took the company off track of the project with the most momentum. Then we had to start from scratch. What I mentioned to the executive was simply an idea in the works. I had developed a logo and a website for the project because I always like to have a visual piece of artwork associated with my projects, more for personal reasons than for industry reasons. Laura was excited about the project and said she wanted to read the script right away. She said she wanted it shipped to her East Coast office or e-mailed to her ASAP.

I was thinking to myself, "There's just one problem, it's just an idea. Yikes!"

In other words, I hadn't written the script yet. Of course, I didn't say that.

I said what any driven entrepreneur says, "No problem!"

I also mentioned that the script is going through some fine tuning, but as soon as it is 'finalized' she will be the first to read it. The meeting went well overall, but basically I had completely lost the focus on *Hollywood Chaos* and then went off having to write a script for another project.

Prior to starting that script, I dissolved the *Hollywood Chaos* team and thanked everyone for their time and commitment. I let them know that if the script ever came into fruition, they would be the first to be considered for production positions. During our last meeting, I bought everyone a lotto ticket. The idea being that breaking into Hollywood is like winning the lotto. I made them promise that if they won, they had to split it with me. They all agreed, and we parted ways on a sad but positive note.

I was then off to write the next script, *The Diva and the*

Princess. I took a few days to brainstorm the concept and fully flush out the plot and story. I wondered if the executive was seriously interested in the script, or if she was just kind of saying that to be polite. A day or two after my wonderment, I received an e-mail from her asking for the script. I told her that she would have it in within two weeks. I couldn't believe I was promising such a thing and I didn't even have an outline or anything for the script yet. But this was an opportunity I couldn't afford to miss out on.

At the time, I was working at another public relations marketing firm. I took off a week for personal reasons, i.e., to focus on writing the script. To my surprise, I finished the first draft in one week. I gave it to my A-list team to read and obtain feedback. Then I made edits and finishing touches. The second draft had to become my final draft because my two weeks were up. I e-mailed the script to the executive, and I continued to follow-up. After a few weeks, I heard back from her saying she loved the script and my writing, but it had to be read and approved by others in the company, particularly their producing team who was actually going to select the movies for their production slate. After weeks and weeks of anxiously waiting, I started to lose faith, which is another lesson. Never lose faith in yourself, your projects, your team or anything!

The minute I lost faith was the minute projects seem to dissolve. I never heard back from anyone at the company. I only discovered what project they ended up producing based on reading about it in the trades. Unfortunately, their film selection ended up bombing completely at the theaters. They should have gone with *Hollywood Chaos* or *The Diva and the Princess.* Their profits couldn't have been any worse than what they were for the film they chose to produce. To the company's defense, maybe the film wasn't that bad (which I to this day purposely have not seen). Maybe the movie failed due to the distribution company not putting in enough PA (prints and advertising) money toward the film. In that scenario, whether they chose my film or other film, without the correct marketing strategy and marketing dollars behind a film, it is difficult for any film to sustain itself in theaters.

While it is always important to take control of your career and to be a risk-taker, you've got to take smart calculated risks. Don't let the chaos in Hollywood get you off track of your original pursuit. Remain passionate and persistent. Focus on one project at a time. If multi-tasking is more your style, it must be done with excellence.

FouRTeeN

An Agent for Good

One morning, I received a phone call from my friend Maria. I had just finished a tasty cinnamon raisin bagel from Noah's on Ventura Boulevard. I was out taking my 5-month-old son for a ride in his stroller.

When I answered my cell, Maria asked vibrantly, "Why is my good friend on the front cover of *Back Stage West*?"

I was very confused by what she was saying. She is from Bilbao, Spain and although she speaks fluent English very well, sometimes she says things in an odd way. I wasn't sure if she was really asking me, or if it was a rhetorical question.

"Who? Which friend is on there?" I inquired.

"You, silly!" she said.

I could tell she thought I was trying to be funny, but I wasn't sure why.

"I'm serious. Who is on the cover?" I said in a non-joking manner.

"You!" she exclaimed.

"Huh, me? What are you talking about?" I asked.

"You didn't know?" she replied.

"Know what?" I said

"I am drinking a cup of tea and pulled out my *Back Stage West* to read, and you, my friend, are on the front cover!" she screamed into the phone.

"What? What do you mean I am on the front cover?" I asked again, still very confused.

She said, "Your picture is on the front cover. You look beautiful."

At this point I still had no clue what she was talking about. "Maria, are you joking? I don't understand," I said.

She started cracking up hysterically and we both started laughing.

She replied, "I'm not kidding. Go to a newsstand and you'll see what I'm saying. You are on the front cover of *Back Stage West* with a caption that says, 'An Agent for Good.' There's an entire article about you. They had to interview you to get such detailed information. You must have forgotten."

"Ohhh! Yes, a writer from *Back Stage* did interview me several weeks ago, but I thought it was for some kind of blurb for the Actorfest program since I am a speaker this year," I explained.

"Sweetie, this is more than just a blurb. You gotta go get it right now and buy a bunch of copies. I can't believe you, my great friend, are on the front cover. This is wonderful. Call me after you read it."

As I headed to the newsstand on the corner of Van Nuys Blvd. and Ventura Blvd., I texted a few of my friends about it. I told them to go get a copy of the newspaper, even though I hadn't even seen it yet.

My friend Mary Nicole, the actress, called and said, "Angela, this is it! You have made it! Girrrrl, you have broken into Hollywood!"

"Mary, you are hilarious!" I said.

"Seriously, honey, there isn't much better than this—the front page of *Back Stage*. That's my girl!" she exclaimed.

I understood where she was coming from because she was just excited about it. We all were. I bought a stack of papers from the newsstand. When I got home, I sat down to read it as my baby took a nap. After I finished, I immediately e-mailed the author, Sarah Kuhn, about the article. I thanked her for the publicity and for the well-written article. I certainly did not expect to be on the front cover, nevertheless have a full-page feature article about me. It was definitely a moment I look back on and smile. Sometimes when I am feeling stressed about my career or life in general, I read it and get inspired. Hopefully it can ignite a spark in you as well.

***

Actorfest Profile
A Helping Hand
Agent Angela M. Hutchinson gives back to her entertainment community.
By Sarah Kuhn, *Back Stage West* - October 10, 2008

Angela M. Hutchinson is always on the lookout for fresh talent. As a theatrical and commercial agent at RPM Talent Agency, a Los Angeles-based boutique firm, she attends theatre, filters through referrals from trusted sources, and has even spotted a few folks with print-work potential at the local mall. She honed these handy actor-spotting skills as the founder of Breaking into Hollywood (*www.breakingintohollywood.org*), a nonprofit organization that helps those in the entertainment industry achieve their career goals. "The whole point is connecting people, matching people with their needs," she says. "A director might call me and say, 'I'm looking for this type of [actor]; do you know anyone who might be interested?' They would come to me knowing that through [our] membership we have some strong actors."

It was her work with the nonprofit that led Hutchinson to the business of agenting. "We had a panel discussion on how to get representation—a panel of agents," she remembers. "One of the agents ended up discovering one of the actors at the event and was like, 'You have a great eye for picking talent. We're actually looking for a new agent right now. Would you be interested?' I ended up interviewing with the owner of the agency, and we got along."

This was a new path for Hutchinson, who had moved to Hollywood to pursue her writing career. She penned four screenplays, networked with other industry pros, and served as president of the Scriptwriters Network. And yet, around 2005, she started to feel disenchanted with the business. "I had gotten to a point in my career where I felt like I wasn't where I needed to be as a writer," she says. "I thought, I've [taken] all the right steps. This should equal success. What's going on? When I talked to my mother, she said, 'Are you giving back?' I said, 'Of course I am. I do a lot of things in the community to give back.' And she said, 'No, are you giving back in the field you want to be successful in?' I thought, Hmm." Hutchinson pauses, breaking into a chuckle. "No."

Inspired, Hutchinson started Breaking into Hollywood, which hosts various panel discussions and events for those looking to jump-start their careers. She still dedicates a good amount of time to the organization, and she's thrilled that her work as an agent gives her yet another opportunity to help actors get started in the industry. When pitching her clients for projects, she tries to keep her approach respectful and succinct. "Generally I know the casting director I'm pitching to," she says. "So it's really just a matter of shooting over an e-mail and letting them know why I think my client is suited [for the role]. I'm really big on e-mail, because I think it's less imposing on the person. I know the person is just as busy as I am, so to get a million phone calls can be annoying. But an e-mail they can read at their leisure."

When scouting talent, Hutchinson takes a few things into consideration. She's a big fan of training, as it shows passion for the craft. She also likes to know that the actor is focused and dedicated to the long process of career building. "I find that most actors do not know if they want to be in film or TV, which is really important to me," she says. "It's okay to do both, but you've got to start somewhere, and most actors just say, 'Oh, whatever comes.' I think it's important to know where [you want to start], because that helps me, as your agent, to target more of those roles for you."

That said, she also takes notice when actors have extra assets in their arsenals. "That's another thing I look for: someone who has another background aside from acting," she says. "If they sing, if they dance—some other strong skill set that's very marketable."

The agent recalls finding one such actor while speaking at a panel discussion. "She's a comedian," says Hutchinson. "And her question was something along the lines of, 'Is it okay for me to be pursuing my career as a comedian, or should I just tell you as an agent I'm an actor?' Sometimes an actor comes into my office, and they'll say they're a writer-director-producer and an actor. That's not attractive to me—that they're pursuing four different careers. So I thought that was a good question to address." But because being a comedian ties in neatly with the pursuit of acting and because this actor was very focused on her craft, Hutchinson saw the extra skill as a marketable asset. "And," she says with a chuckle, "she made me laugh."

Hutchinson enjoys her work as an agent, assisting actors in achieving their dreams, but that doesn't mean she has forgotten her own dream. On the writing side, she has published a children's book titled "Charm Kids" and has a forthcoming tome related to her nonprofit. She says she has put the scriptwriting on the back burner —but not forever. "That's something I [still] want to pursue but a little bit after I master my agent career," she says. "Right now I'm building the toolbox."

***

After reading my interview in *Back Stage*, for a moment I forgot that the article was about me. I was actually taking in the information and knowledge as if someone else was being interviewed. I liked the ending quote about the toolbox. One of my mentee's father actually coined that phrase, and it really stuck with me. I find that analogy a realistic one to remember when you think about building your career for the long-term. Even if you are trying to have a one hit wonder career or become a reality TV star with that credit as your only claim to fame, I still suggest creating a toolbox. No matter what level, having a box of tools is necessary to master the art, the craft and the business.

Prior to my feature cover story in *Back Stage*, I was asked to participate in their "Ask an Agent" column. I often contributed by providing an answer to the question they posed. Below are my responses, which hopefully will provide insight into the industry, particularly for actors.

***

Will you do something that benefits your client but for, which you'll receive no pay?
by Sarah Kuhn, *Back Stage West* - January 29, 2009

Angela M. Hutchinson, *Theatrical and Commercial agent, RPM Talent Agency, Los Angeles*

"Yes. For the clients who I believe have the potential to go the furthest in this industry, I will occasionally do things that benefit them even if I don't receive actual payment, because I am committed to their long-term careers. Some examples might be researching classes and events that I think they should attend, or I might set up general meetings with casting directors.

For one of my clients, I set up a meeting with a talented B-list director who has worked with Angela Bassett and many other celebrities. I thought my client and the director would get along on a personal level, since they're both from Chicago like me. So I set up an informal meeting where I was present to introduce them and simply chit chat about life, the industry, and upcoming projects. The two really hit it off well and made plans to play basketball and watch a football game. Unfortunately, my client moved back to Chicago temporarily, so he's unable to hang out with the director. But at least the director likes my client (and vice versa) on a personal level, which will come in handy when he's directing a movie and there is a role that is perfect for my client. Or when my client blows up to an A-lister and he's in a position to select the director he wants to work with, he will remember this director's initial hospitality.

I am not an agent because of the money. Eventually a lot of money can be made in agenting, but if I were really into making money, I would have just pursued my engineering career. Instead, I decided to pursue my passion for working in entertainment. I will always be committed to helping my clients and fellow industry pros achieve their Hollywood dreams, even if I never get paid for it. I am all about 'paying it forward' -- I love that movie."

Is the Digital Age Hurting the Actor-Agent Relationship?
by Sarah Kuhn, *Back Stage West* - May 7, 2008

Angela M. Hutchinson, *Theatrical and Commercial agent, RPM Talent Agency, Los Angeles*
"I do not believe that the actor-agent relationship is suffering because of the digital revolution. If anything, electronic communication enables me to spend more time working on my client's behalf. If an actor would like to have more communication with his or her agent than the agent is providing, the actor should consider signing with another agent who shares the talent's viewpoint. I think it is difficult to maintain a healthy business relationship if the actor and agent are not on the same

page as it relates to effective communication.

I am usually quite sensitive to the mindset of actors, but I have to say that actors should spend less time worried about communicating with their agents and focus more on accomplishing their career goals. Many times, actors find excuse after excuse to fault something or someone for their lack of success. I think it is important for actors to embrace the digital revolution and find ways to strengthen the relationship with their agent and manager via personal websites, MySpace, Youtube, Facebook, [Twitter, TED,] blogs, etc. The digital revolution is providing actors with an opportunity to take more control of their careers. Actors should take advantage of our technologically advancing society.

If an actor is talented, trained, and tenacious and continues to book audition after audition, I am positive the agent will not forget about the client and the relationship is far from suffering. As we speak, the agent is probably using electronic communication to secure the talent's next gig, which may very well be a national SAG webisode that pays $20,000."

Sending Out Actors Against Type
by Sarah Kuhn, *Back Stage West* - January 30, 2008

Angela M. Hutchinson, *Theatrical and Commercial agent, RPM Talent Agency, Los Angeles*
"I often send clients out on auditions against type, because my job is to help the casting and production team find the best actors for their project. However, my decision to submit against type usually depends on the casting director -- whether or not I know their preferences. If I do not know the CD personally, then I base my submission decision on the descriptiveness of the character breakdown. Some CDs are very specific and want agents to submit exact matches to the breakdown, which is understandable, because CDs often have direct orders from the director or producers. Other CDs -- the ones that ultimately go on to be producers -- ask agents to be creative with our submissions. In that case, I always do that.

From time to time, I will also submit [a woman] for a role that specifies male, depending on my gut feeling about the role or based on the overall vision of the project and creative team involved. Also, sometimes the hardest submissions are submitting fairly young actors for an older role. I have a 23-year-old client who nailed an audition for the role of a 37-year-old woman who had a teenage daughter. When she was informed about booking the role, she questioned whether or not to accept it, because she was disappointed that the industry saw her much older than her real age. Eventually she got over it and did an excellent job with her performance. The age issue usually just comes up with my female clients and from time to time with a few males. Either way, I try not to worry about how an actor feels about a certain role, because I am by no means a psychologist. As an agent, my primary responsibility is to submit, pitch, and book my clients, regardless of how they feel about playing a certain role -- unless it goes against their moral principles. Also, I determine, which of my clients to submit for a role based on his or her overall career objectives."

End of Pilot Season as We Know It
Actors benefit as networks shift to yearlong rollout.
by Nicole Kristal, *Back Stage West* - April 18, 2008

Telecommuting
Talent agent Angela M. Hutchinson of RPM Talent Agency said, "Although tape submissions have become slightly more acceptable due to the digital age, nothing can replace seeing an actor audition live in a room." Hutchinson represents L.A. actors only and said ultimately it's up to individuals whether they come to the city for pilot season or submit on tape, though she always recommends that her clients audition in person.

Will you take a chance on an actor with few or no credits?
by Sarah Kuhn, *Back Stage West* - August 15, 2008

Angela M. Hutchinson, *Theatrical and Commercial agent,*
RPM Talent Agency, Los Angeles
"I am always open to accepting a talented and committed actor with few credits, but I would never sign an actor with absolutely no credits, not even a child actor. Aside from the typical film/ TV credits, other acceptable credits can be in community theatre, short films, corporate videos, etc. Although I would sign

an actor with few credits, I am typically interested in actors with strong credits who can command the room during an audition, which can be determined based on the presence they have with me during our initial representation meeting.

The other item of importance when I consider signing new talent to my roster is a committed actor —one who is dedicated to a long-term career in acting. I am not interested in creating a star or celebrity as much as I am interested in developing a non-working/aspiring actor into a consistently working and respected actor.

As a bit of advice on how to obtain credits if you have no credits, start submitting for even unpaid jobs with student films and independent shorts, as well as plays. Having a body of known credits helps the casting team determine the range of the actor. But nothing surpasses an actor nailing the lines in the audition room. Oh, and I should mention that having other talents and skills in terms of athletics, singing, languages — those are also important to me when I consider signing an actor with few credits.

If you have no credits, you do not need to be focused on getting an agent. You need to hustle in Hollywood. Network, network, network! Build somewhat of a résumé and maybe even a reel before attempting to sign with an agent. As a final thought, whether you have no credits, few credits, or tons of credits but do not have an agent and can't seem to find one after putting your all into it, don't worry, it will come in due time. Do not let not having an agent be a hindrance to you pursuing your acting career. An agent makes 10 percent; you make 90 percent. Be sure you are doing 90 percent of the work now. I can almost guarantee if you are doing the 90 percent, the agent will find you or you will find him/her when it's your season."

***

As an agent, I spoke on a variety of panels for *Back Stage*'s Actorfest, the Showbiz Expo, film festivals and youth showcases. I was also interviewed by *Focus Online Magazine*. Hopefully you will find the following transcription from the live interview informative.

***

Interview with Angela M. Hutchinson
Talent Agent for RPM Talent Agency
By Maurice Poplar, *Focus Online Magazine*

This month, I had the pleasure of interviewing Angela M.
Hutchinson, a very savvy Hollywood Insider cum talent agent.
I'm very grateful she made time to shed some light on the L.A.
Agent Market. Angela works for RPM Talent Agency. They
represent Actors, both non-union and SAG (Screen Actor's
Guild Union).

MP: Angela, start off by telling me about RPM.
AH: The agency has been around for about five years. We've
been SAG franchised for two years. SAG franchised means
that we have the ability to represent SAG actors. I run the print
modeling department and the kid's commercial department. In
addition, I have about twelve actors that I'm representing; some
across the board both theatrical and commercial. Whether it's
either or, depends on the need of the actor.

MP: What do you look for in new talent?
AH: A lot of agents like to have people come in and read
for them, see what they've done or take a look at their reel. I
think reels are important, but for me it's much more about the
personality of the person, how aggressive they are because I'm
an aggressive agent. I need the talent to be just as aggressive.
Their resume needs to look very together. Also, L.A. Casting
and Actor's Access, which are the services that we use to get the
break downs for all the roles, they need to already be on there,
submitting themselves.

MP: And those are websites, right?
AH: Those are websites, *lacasting.com* and *actorsaccess.com*.

MP: So do you go out personally looking for talent? How do
you find them?
AH: I've just joined the agency, so it's been through personal
contacts that I've been adding new people to my roster.

MP: Other than aggressive, how would you describe a good

candidate to get an agent?

AH: Someone who has a theater background. That shows you have a passion for acting. A lot of times I've asked actors, "Have you done theater?" and they'll say, "Oh, I'm really not into theater." Well, you must not really be into acting [is what I think of an actor who says that]. Theater is a great way to showcase your self. That's how it all started [live stage plays before motion pictures]. Not that you have to constantly be in plays, but you should have a background in them.

For me, it's also, do you want to be a film actor or TV actor. A lot of times you ask people, "What's your goal?" As an agent, I'm supposed to be on your team, to help you along with your publicist and your manager and whoever else you may have. So I'll say, 'What's your plan for your life? Are you gonna be a film actor or a TV actor?' Sometimes they're just like both, "Or doesn't matter. Whatever happens, happens. I just want to act." That's the wrong attitude. "You have to know where you're going, TV or film. You can say both, but I prefer for someone to know where they're going, otherwise, I can't help you get there.

MP: Let's talk about the SAG / Non-SAG worlds.

AH: The difference between SAG and Non-Union is the type of project. There is a lot of non-union work out there. Commercials, student films, short films and even some full length feature films are non-union. The SAG projects are all network TV, cable TV, and studio feature films; those are all SAG projects. Being SAG is important, but you don't want to try to get SAG if you haven't really exhausted the non-union world. For the non-union actor, there is work out there. Try to get that work. Get in those student films and short films and build your non-union side of your resume. Then when it's time, you can attempt to get SAG.

You can get vouchers, you need three of them. You can become a member of AFTRA (American Federation of TV and Radio Artists), another association and after a year you can join SAG, I think. Or you can be Taft Hartley'd (a waiver-invitation into SAG) to be in a commercial, in a film or TV show.

MP: Do you have any advice for young vying actors out there?

AH: Just make sure it's what you really want to do in life. There are a lot of other careers that provide high income. If you are going into acting to try to get paid well or become famous, that would not be the reason to do it. The reason to go into acting is because it's your God-given passion. If you feel it's what you are on this planet to do. If that's not the case, it's not worth going through all the rejection, pain and other obstacles you will endure along the way to your victory. Just make sure it's what you want to do.

***

Working as an agent was rewarding. I helped several actors go from non-union to SAG. I also received notoriety in the industry among fellow colleagues including casting directors, producers, directors and actors. However, I often felt like a glamorized car salesman. Nothing is wrong with being a car salesman; it's just not the job for me.

Whenever I feel disinterested in my career, I seek out advice from mentors. After an informational meeting I had with a casting director, my interest piqued in yet another career path within the industry. You guessed it ... casting! The original purpose of meeting with my casting director mentor was for her to give me advice on how to book my actor clients for more auditions and how to pitch talent more effectively as an agent. Toward the end of the conversation, I inquired about her casting experiences. She openly shared with me her colorful stories as a seasoned casting director. Right there inside Starbucks as I shooed away a fly from my infant son, I was bit by the casting bug.

FiFTeeN
Casting Diaries

After being a talent agent for two years, I decided to transition into casting. A contributing factor that helped me make a smooth transition was attending an event my non-profit organization hosted titled, "Greenlight Your Showbiz Career." While observing the filming of the event's promo video, I was talking with actress/producer Tangi Miller in the green room. She was one of the event's panelist, and an excellent speaker. The organization wanted to capture her advice on camera for those trying to break into Hollywood. While she was waiting her turn to be interviewed, my best friend Sarah and I casually talked with her about the industry. Tangi gave us the inside scoop about her upcoming movie she had recently produced and also starred in, alongside Malik Yoba (the black cop from "New York Undercover"). Ironically, Malik's co-star, Michael DeLorenzo (the Puerto Rican cop on the show), was a panelist for the BiH event that day. Michael and Tangi spoke on the "True Hollywood Stories" panel, which was geared toward industry veterans sharing their experiences with aspiring professionals.

While in the green room, Tangi mentioned that she was preparing to produce another feature film within the next few months. I immediately informed her that I was making a transition from agenting to casting. I told her to contact me if she needed a casting assistant or someone to help her casting director. She said we should definitely connect soon. I sent her a follow-up e-mail a few days later. The following week, we met in Larchmont Park at a Jamba Juice to discuss her film. She had such a delightful personality. We talked for over an hour about the last films she had produced and some of her production and casting nightmares. I assured her that hiring me to cast her film would be far from a bad experience. Toward the end of our conversation, she offered me the job as the main casting director. I was excited about being given an opportunity to work with established actors on a feature film as the sole casting director.

Working with Tangi and her company, Olivia Entertainment, was an amazing experience. I was definitely in the trenches on the casting end and sometimes on the production side. The cast and crew were very close-knit; everyone gave their all.

The casting process for the film was fairly simple. First, I released a character breakdown of all the roles. Then, I created talent lists based on interested actors and producers' picks. Tangi and the other producers primarily wanted name talent for the lead and co-star roles, but they were open to having rising actors in the secondary roles.

Surprisingly, many of the name actors' agents were easy to deal with and not nearly as *Hollywood* as often perceived. We had a few kinks, but for the most part all went well. An enlightenment was learning that it isn't always about the money for attaching a celebrity actor to a film. Since this was an ultra-low budget (ULB) SAG-indie film, the actors weren't going to get paid big bucks. Even so, several established television actors were interested in landing a role in Tangi's film. They were focused on gaining film credits and enhancing their portfolio to establish themselves as a film actor. Also, they may have had an interest in working with a rising producer like Tangi because she could very well employ them in the future for higher paying roles.

The first movie I cast was called, *Guardian of Eden.* The main cast included Tangi Miller ("Tyler Perry's Madea's Family Reunion"), Persia White ("Girlfriends"), David Ramsey ("Dexter"), and other name actors. I visited the set twice. One day when I was there they decided to put my baby boy in a hospital scene to make it more realistic. Alexander had his first film debut. Previously, he had his first industry job when he booked and filmed a Gerber viral video. Although it was never released, he still got paid for it. That job allowed me to set up his Coogan's bank account, which minors working in the entertainment business must have, but can only open after receiving a professional acting job.

A few weeks after we wrapped production on *Guardian of Eden*, Tangi called me and asked if I was up for casting another movie. Of course I was, but she made it clear there were some crazy time constraints. We had about one week to have the whole film cast—about 20 roles in all. With a team effort, we made it happen.

Unlike the first film, we did not hold auditions. This time it was strictly based off actors whose work we were familiar with already. We ended up casting actors that either she or I knew personally. Casting this second film was a great opportunity for me to give roles to talented actor friends and colleagues. For some of the roles that had not yet been filled, we did release a small breakdown. Often, this is how casting happens for films. The producing team selects the main cast. Then, the casting director releases secondary or last minute written in one-liner roles on the breakdowns. Agents submit their clients and unrepresented actors submit themselves, then the audition occurs.

Once production began on the film, the casting and booking process was a little more chaotic than the first film I cast for Olivia Entertainment. Still it was an enlightening experience working for Tangi and alongside her. She is the type of producer that allows you to be creative in your job, but also provides specific direction and thoughts on her desires. She communicates with sophistication and style, which is something I admire. I am thankful to Tangi for giving me my first casting director job.

After casting her two films, I went on to cast another film with Ben Foster, a rising teen director who filmed his first feature length movie after directing and producing several short films. Next, I cast the pick-up shots for a comedy film. They had already filmed the movie but needed to add a new scene. I didn't have to hold auditions because I selected the cast from the pool of talented actors whom I already knew.

For my next casting gig, I was hired to attach the main talent for a feature film. The producer wanted to have attachments to help him secure financing. This was my first time taking on such an assignment. Even though it was not an easy task, the money was well worth it and I knew I could do it. Within a few weeks, I fulfilled my commitment of attaching four prominent actors from the producer's approved talent list.

Most impressive was being able to secure a signed letter of intent (LOI) from a William Morris Endeavor repped actor. This is often unheard of because name actors don't like to attach themselves to projects for the purpose of securing financing. Reason being is if the money needed to produce the film is not able to be secured using an actor with a name, it could bring down the value of their name. I understand that concept, but I also disagree with it depending on the situation. If the investors are well-connected within the industry, it might not be the best strategy. However, if the investors are professional athletes, bankers or other people that aren't so connected with the industry, I think it is okay to take a chance at least one or twice with attaching talent to secure financing.

In addition to casting films, I have cast a live-action superhero web-series. Later, I went on to cast several short film thesis projects at American Film Institute. I was referred to the students by one of my mentors, Marie Cantin, who was a Co-Producer for *Save the Last Dance* and Production Manager for *Collateral*.

Casting a short film with students as the producers and directors was a unique experience. Each of the producing teams I worked with handled their casting sessions with a distinct style. I enjoyed working with different personality types because it enabled me to become a better communicator, further enhancing my toolbox.

My casting experiences allowed me to not only learn more about another aspect of the entertainment industry, but also gave me the opportunity to help talented actors accomplish their goals of booking roles. Although I didn't actually keep a daily casting diary, I learned lots of lessons.

14 Auditioning Tips for Aspiring Actors

1) *Don't bring food into the casting room.* Sounds like common sense, right? Believe it or not, an actor once brought an entire McDonald's value meal inside the room. Then, he had the nerve to

apologize as he ate it during his audition. That is just an absolute no-no. My casting assistant almost burst into laughter. It was definitely funny, but also very rude and disrespectful of the actor, especially since he didn't even offer a French fry.

2) *Always have your sides.* Even if you are off book, meaning you have memorized your lines, it is still a good idea to have your sides in your hand during the audition. The best actors that truly know their lines turn the pages to their sides without actually looking at the paper. Having the sides present is always a good idea because on rare occasion the writer may be in the room and it will show respect for their work.

3) *Stick with the lines.* Writers and producers work hard on fine tuning a script. For an actor to come in the room and dice up the lines with their own words is very annoying. Sometimes, it may be appropriate if the script has incorrect grammar or a mistake. If a line feels uncomfortable to say, it is sometimes okay to change a word or two. For the most part, it is always best to stick with the script given.

4) *Do not bring a friend in the room or children.* Simply inappropriate and can be a distraction to the casting team.

5) *Do not shake hands with the casting team.* Imagine if the casting director has to audition 50 people that day. He/she does not want to receive the germs of all of those people. A cordial hello or thank you for bringing me in is sufficient.

6) *If you forget a line and don't have your sides with you, just say "Line."* The casting assistant/ reader will give you your next line. No need to get flustered.

7) *Don't ask to start the scene over.* If you mess up on a line or two, just keep going. If you would like to start over, it's best to just start over instead of asking. If you ask and the casting director says, "No," you'll likely leave your audition feeling embarrassed. To start over, just politely state you are going to start over, or just do it. The best way to recover from a mistake is to continue on with your lines. Plenty of actors have messed up their lines during an audition and were still invited to callbacks. The casting team is not focused on the mistakes an actor makes, but the overall delivery of their performance.

8) *When finishing a scene, either say "Scene!" or just stop.* Don't continue to ad lib unless the lines you are saying brilliantly fit with the script. Actors often ad lib to a scene with stupid lines, which takes away from the performance the actor just delivered.

9) *Dress like the character, but don't go overboard.* If you are auditioning for the role of a teacher, surely don't come dressed like a stripper. For a doctor, a white lab coat is appropriate. However, if you are auditioning for a fireman, no need to rent a bulky fireman uniform. Ask your acting coach for tips on appropriate dress for your auditions, or just use your common sense and instincts. If you have neither, maybe get a book on developing that part of yourself. Otherwise, you might consider selecting another career. A great actor must have great instincts and common sense.

10) *If you are late, don't blame it on traffic.* If you are late, you can apologize but no need to give the reason. An actor looks quite silly when the casting director just saw 50 actors on time, and then one claims he/she is late due to traffic, or not finding parking, or going to the wrong audition room. Apologize for your tardiness and deliver an amazing performance.

11) *Don't ask for instructions if you don't plan to follow them.* This happens more often than not where an actor wants to know their frame, which is the room space they can use within the camera's frame. Then, after being provided with the requested information, they disregard it and go completely out of frame. One time during a casting session, an actor asked me if he could use a chair. I expressed to him the importance of standing since that's how the scene would be filmed. He went on to explain he practiced his lines at home while sitting on a chair. Then, he grabbed a chair against my instruction, and auditioned sitting down. Of course he did not get a callback. He did however display his lack of ability to listen and follow instructions. Actors must absolutely be able to take direction inside the casting room. Often, the director is present during the audition and uses that time to determine the actor's ability to be directed.

12) *Don't hesitate to ask questions about the script, story or characters, but don't be too inquisitive.* It shows an actor is well prepared when one asks a relevant question about the character's personality or the scene. But it can be annoying if an actor asks too many questions about the character's journey or makes non-relevant comments about the scene.

13) *For a callback, look the same.* Don't drastically change your look including hair color, hair style, or even clothes. For a callback, most actors wear the same or similar outfit and style their hair the same way. This is smart. Obviously, there is something the casting team liked about an actor if invited to callbacks. But likely, the actor will never know exactly why they were selected to audition again. If the actor changes one factor in the equation, it may decrease chances of being liked again. Something as minor as a hair style could affect an actor landing a

role. I can recall an actress who wore her hair down for the initial audition, and then for the callback she had a ponytail. The producer thought she looked too young. Now, you might think the producer would just ask the actress to take down her ponytail. It's not the producer's job to figure out why an actor looked older before and now looks too young. It's the actor's job to be consistent throughout the audition process.

14) *Always bring your headshot AND resume, even for the callback.* Would you show up to a job interview without a resume? I hope not! Same scenario with acting. Also, don't ask to borrow a stapler to attach your resume to your headshot. Come into the casting room prepared, or best not to come at all.

SiXTeeN

T4

Breaking into Hollywood is about Teamwork, Timing, Talent and Tenacity. You may have moved to Los Angeles either a few months ago or within the last five years, or maybe you are a native of California or have been living here for over ten years. No matter how long you have been pursuing your entertainment career, your vision is likely the same as your fellow industry colleagues: to see your creative vision come to pass; to make lots of money; to entertain; and/or influence the world to change by making a political or social statement.

The point is, there are over hundreds of thousands of writers, actors, musicians, directors (or whatever it is you are pursuing) in the world, and most reside here in Los Angeles or New York. So, why should you be the success story? Is it because you are the best singer? Why should someone choose your script over someone else? Why should you get the role over another great actor? Why do things happen the way they do in Hollywood? The answers to those questions are ones we could all attempt to provide, but the fact is no human being really knows. Instead of driving yourself crazy over this industry, you can leave the insanity by remembering **T4**.

Teamwork
As an artistic professional, it is important to have a group of people who can be somewhat accountable for your decisions throughout your career pursuit. This can be established with friends, mentors, family members, religious/political leaders, or colleagues. A writer must be able to accept criticism and

take candid feedback. Writing is a collaborative effort. You've seen the names during the closing credits. Develop your team now. In other words, find the people in the business whom you want to work with and stay faithful to them. Aspiring producers often focus on trying to reach the famous. But yesterday's Julia Roberts is today's Lindsey Lohan or tomorrow's Alyssa Marie (who is that?—my point exactly). Create your own clique, or at least join forces with a team of people who can help you reach the caliber of those who you currently would like to work with in the industry.

Timing

We can all agree when preparation meets opportunity, success occurs. Remember, a career takes time to develop. Yes, it may be shorter or much longer from one person to another, but pursuing a career in showbiz is a journey. Therefore, it is vital to develop a written action plan of your specific goals on a short-term (weekly), mid-term (1 year) and long-term (10+years) basis.

It's just like writing a script or taking a road trip. You must know where you are going before you get there. Being confident in your plan will help keep you on track and focused on your goals, rather than comparing yourself to others. If it is meant for you to be a writer and have your screenplay produced, or be an A-list actress, your time WILL come! Instead of hanging in there, stand strongly rooted in your plan and be sure to plant seeds by helping others along their journey.

Talent

You've heard the saying, "the cream of the crop, will rise to the top." That may hold true to some degree. From the words of my wise mother, there will always be someone better looking than you, more intelligent than you, more qualified than you. The point of life is not to be the best, but to be the best YOU can be in everything you do.

Make sure you are enrolled in classes to perfect your craft, network, actively join groups and socialize with people that can help you take your career to the next level. Most importantly, be sure you are learning the business side of the industry area you are pursuing. Talent does not just involve craft. One must not only have a passion for the craft, but also a thorough understanding of the business, especially to become an award-winning success story.

Tenacity
Before I go on to explain the importance of NEVER quitting, let me first address the importance of making sure this is the calling for your life. Don't stand in the way of someone else's opportunity. Once you have determined your dream is the thing you love and want to pursue, do what the poem below says.

DON'T QUIT!
When things go wrong as they sometimes will,
When the road you're trudging seems all up hill,
When the funds are low and the debt is high,
And you want to smile, but you have to sigh,
When care is pressing you down a bit,
Rest if you must, but don't you quit.

Life is queer with its twists and turns,
As everyone of us sometimes learns,
And many a failure turns about,
When he might have won had he stuck it out.
Don't give up though the pace seems slow,
You may succeed with another blow.

Success is failure turned inside out,
The silver tint of the clouds of doubt,
And you never can tell how close you are,
It may be near when it seems so far.
So stick to the fight when you're hardest hit,
It's when things seems worst, that you must not quit.
~Author Unknown

You must continue to have faith and believe in your dreams, and not just for you, but for the generations to come. Imagine if Steven Spielberg, Oprah Winfrey, Bill Gates, Donald Trump, Michael Jordan or Calvin Klein had quit. Think of how many more people would currently be unemployed or how you and I would have never been exposed to their creative talents.

My belief is tenacity is the most important of **T4**. If you have the talent and the team, but you give up before the timing, you may never experience your dream. **You can't break into Hollywood or any industry if you quit!**

SeVeNTeeN

Power Lines

While living in the South Bay area with the crazy roommate who stole my identity, I for the first time was exposed to shoes dangling by their laces over power lines. I had never seen such a thing in any neighborhood where I lived. I wondered what kind of person would throw their shoe up there. Then, one day I got home early from work and saw kids in the street having what look to be like a competition of who could throw their shoes the highest and get them to land on the power lines. It was quite sad to see children resort to such a mindless activity. However, it seemed to bring joy to their faces, and for that it made me smile. In the city of Torrance, I noticed there were so many power lines within the neighborhood streets. However, when I went to work and drove through Beverly Hills and into Century City, I hardly saw power lines. I wondered where their power lines were in those more elite communities. Clearly, every city needed power to function.

When I arrived at work one day, I started surfing the web and researching the topic of power lines. I discovered a lot of theories, one of which was the fact many affluent communities had their power lines either neatly placed behind their houses or businesses, or buried entirely underground. Both options were more expensive than having them built in front of one's house like the Torrance community where I was living at the time. Some of the research I found about power lines talked about the dangers of the electromagnetic radiation that can be emitted from the lines within a certain distance, particularly from the power substations, which is the main power source to the power lines.

I wondered if the kids could be affected by playing near the power lines every day, perhaps causing some minor damage to their brain or learning ability. I thought about the movies, *Erin Brockovich* and *Civil Action*. In those communities, the contaminated water caused the local citizens health problems. The concept of power lines really drew my interest causing me to research the topic more in depth. The studies and facts I found were astonishing. Many documents supported the idea that living near power lines and being exposed to local power substations could cause brain cancer, along with other problems like miscarriages. There were also studies that disproved the theory of power lines being able to affect the community. While both sides were convincing, I was more intrigued by the idea that those children who lived near power lines could possibly have or develop more health or mental problems than those in wealthier areas that had underground power lines.

I printed over 100 pages of documentation from the Internet on the subject of power lines and health risks. I became totally fascinated with the information and thought one day this could make a great movie. A few months later, I wrote a screenplay about it, inspired by several true stories. Now, you may be wondering why I chose to talk about power lines in a book about breaking into Hollywood.

You may be thinking what in the world does pursuing a dream in Hollywood have to do with power lines. Everything! When you start to think about power lines or the line of power literally, metaphorically or poetically, there is an array of meanings that can be associated with the phrase. An important guideline for someone trying to break into Hollywood is to understand the power source or lines of power to your talent.

For many, the power source may originate from God or some other divine or spiritual element. Some believe the source of power is self. Others may deny the existence of power at all; while some might say power is in us all as a community together. In researching power lines and writing the screenplay, I developed the concept that the line of power starts with you.

If you are an actor or writer striving to make it in Hollywood, it is important to remember you've got the power as the pop group Snap sung it best. In this industry, the idea of an actor having the power over their career is something often preached about, but almost never really implemented. When I worked as an agent, actors felt it was vital to have an agent. It was as if they felt having an agent solely determined their success or their access within the industry. On the contrary, I wanted to work with and represent the powerful actor. I never wanted to be the power source for the actor. I knew if an actor thought I was the missing piece to their puzzle, they were far from understanding Hollywood as I understood it. Therefore, in the end whether my perspective was right or flawed, I knew it wouldn't be an advantageous match. I never represented the powerless actor as I like to identify them.

Powerless Actor Checklist:
1. If I just had an agent ...
2. If I just booked a national commercial ...
3. If I just got Taft Harley-ed or got my SAG card ...
4. If I just booked a co-star role in my favorite TV show ...
5. If I just landed a part in this film ...
6. If I just worked with this director ...
7. If I just got represented by a top manager ...
8. If I just lived in L.A. ...
9. If I could just quit my job ...
10. If I just got the audition ...
11. If I just met the director ...
12. If I just [you fill in the blank!] ...

If, if, if ... You can *what if* this or that all day and all year long! You are where you are because of you. I can almost guarantee the 12 items on the checklist above will not matter to a talented actor who is being 100% persistent and doing everything they can do in their power in terms of:

- Submitting themselves for roles to directors, producers and casting directors
- Attending workshops
- Constantly in acting classes
- Networking at industry events with established professionals
- Getting to know student directors and producers
- Reading books on acting on both the business and the craft

It won't affect or apply to a powerful actor because they are not allowing circumstances to stand in the way. They also do not blame their lack of success on something missing within their self. If you have ever said any, some, or all of the above checklist statements (or similar ones based on your industry), vow to never say or even think them again! Today, vow not to be a powerless professional. Pursue your goals. Sometimes we think just because we say to ourselves or to others around us that we are pursuing our dream, we are actually pursuing it. Pursuing your goal is 100% about action. Stop talking the talk, and start walking the walk.

What happens to many talented individuals that come to Hollywood is they aren't able to persevere through all of the trials and tribulations they face. They lack tenacity—the state of being tenacious—not giving up, no matter what the odds or circumstances presented. I too have been a victim of being *tenaciouslessness*. Here are several ways in which we, as talented individuals, lose our power:

We do not clearly define the source of our power. It's usually not until things go wrong when a writer, actor or singer performs a self-evaluation of their accomplished goals. We must first always understand the source that drives us. Many times we focus on needing an agent or manager, or contract for our next gig rather than the actual source of the power. The source of power is either money, God or self to name a few. What pushes you to excel? What keeps you going when things aren't going your way?

Is it money that drives you, or is it competition, fear, family, God? What is it for you? Figure that out. Then once you know your power source, it will be easier to stay focused on achieving your goals because you can constantly remind yourself of your source. Now of course, if your source is God or faith, that is going to be a more sustaining source of power than money or power itself. Money, power or fame can come and go, but God or your faith is everlasting and unchanging, firmly rooted in principles that have been proven to lead people to victory throughout history. Even though you may define your power as one source, don't be afraid to change your source if you later have a revelation or moment of self-discovery. As long as you have a source, you will be able to move forward. If it's not the accurate source of power, you will discover that eventually and may have to go back to the drawing board to determine the best source for you. Most of the time, having a power source is better than no source at all.

We transfer our power to the wrong line. Allowing our power line to be distracted from its original purpose happens daily in Hollywood. An actor moves to Hollywood to act, but ends up focusing on writing a short because they haven't been successful at getting the auditions they want. They are not as productive, therefore they engage in another industry endeavor thinking that will provide some sense of satisfaction. It's quite possible it may. In my experience I have seen it doesn't, particularly if that actor cannot succeed at the new endeavor. It also happens where a writer clearly wants to write, but becomes frustrated and takes on the hat of producing and directing. Sometimes, it is productive and they are actually able to produce or direct their own movie. However, they often still feel dissatisfied because they have not yet achieved their original goal of selling or optioning a script.

In a meeting I had with a WGA executive, she told me to focus on accomplishing the goals that I had initially set forth to achieve when I first moved out here. She spoke of many WGA members whose goal was to write a film for the purpose of it going to theaters. But when they sold their script and it ended up sitting on a shelf at studio, they became discontent and unfulfilled, even though they had plenty of money in their bank account from the actual sale of the script. She gave another example where a writer is hired to write the first draft of a script. After the script goes through numerous rewrites written by other writers, the first writer is not only unable to recognize their contributions to the movie, but also they may not receive the writing credit for the story or screenplay, which they passionately desired. In a third example, she said writers often get pigeonholed doing writing assignments for various studios. I know many writers, including myself, who would love to get paid top dollars to rewrite a script or even sell a script that never gets made. The point the WGA executive was making was that it's important to always remember your primary goal. You, of course, may have to pay your dues and work in the industry for years before you can accomplish your ideal goals. Along the quest to achieving your dream, keep in mind your main vision. You will feel less content and more empowered.

As for creating your own opportunities, it is great to be entrepreneurial while pursuing a career in Hollywood. It is equally as important to never lose focus of your main goal. Like myself: I moved to L.A. to write. I have had some writing successes such as authoring a published children's picture book and receiving a $25,000 writing assignment, my most financially proud accomplishments as a writer. However, I have not yet achieved my desired success as a screenwriter. To fill that void, I indulged in other areas of the industry that have proven to be productive and successful. I worked as a talent agent and casting director among many other industry hats. Even though I would never take back any of my work experiences, the bottom line is I still desire to achieve my main dream of screenwriting. I transferred my power into other endeavors that produced glamorous results, which made me feel successful and partly is the backbone to me being able to tenaciously continue to pursue my journey.

When you transfer power to another line, it can end up being a very positive experience, no doubt. Likely, it just will not be the exact experience you had envisioned. In some rare cases, a talented individual thinks they want to do one thing, but then when they transfer their power to another line, they realize their passion lies there. That can happen, but typically it happens to those who weren't really confident in what their dream or goal was in the first place. For those of you that firmly know why you came to Hollywood or why you want to move to Hollywood or why you want to pursue whatever dream you have, if you are confident in your dream, it is very important you stay 100% committed to that dream with the ultimate goal of achieving it. Otherwise, you will spend your time having wonderful experiences attached to other power lines, but it will not be your heart's true desires.

We forget to recharge our power lines. Every once in a while, maybe every few months or years, it is necessary for artists to get recharged. We must realize we are not designed

like energizer bunnies, contrary to what you may have been
told about your enthusiasm or work ethic. You must always
take a moment to rejuvenate and clear your head. Usually, we
reorganize our lives when things are slow or not going well. It
can be quite empowering if you do this while in the midst of
success. Why wait for chaos to arise before assessing your goals.
Always be prepared and ready to tackle the next task.

Not recharging your power line leads to a powerless
line. In other words, you may end up burning out before
achieving your dream. Taking excellent care of your health and
mental well-being is necessary. Date, get married, have babies,
adopt children or travel the world, learn a new language or
sport, you get the point. Balance your life and enjoy it! If you
forget to live your life and focus solely on pursuing your dream,
when you achieve it, you will realize you forgot to accomplish
other things that were equally as important to you. Maintaining
a balance throughout your Hollywood pursuit is necessary to
feeling accomplished when you arrive on the red carpet.

We give up our power when our line feels disconnected.
Make a commitment today, right now, within the next minute—
to either regain your power if you feel it's been lost or to preserve
your power. While traveling along your showbiz journey, don't
let Hollywood break you down as you try to break in. Time and
time again throughout my experiences, it was that moment when
I felt like I wanted to give up or break down when I experienced
a breakthrough. The breakthrough was not necessarily the break
I was hoping for, but nonetheless still a valid breakthrough.
These mini breakthroughs kept me sane, confident and
constantly pushing forward.

A celebrity mentor of mine once told me if she had
the kind of tenacity I had, she would be far more successful
than she is now. I thought that was interesting considering how
much I admired her and her achievements. She said she saw
something special in me that I may not be aware of. Yes, that's
a compliment. However, if you don't see in yourself what others
see, it means you are disconnected from your power line. You
can definitely make it in Hollywood without being the most
tenacious or the most talented. But if you aim to be the best
and strive to have the best qualities, you likely won't land too

far from the greatness you are striving to obtain. Making it in
Hollywood may be like winning the lotto, but it doesn't have to
be if you focus on increasing your chances.

One way to increase your odds is to never give up your
power even when you feel like things aren't going your way or
as planned. Reassess, Regroup, Rejuvenate, but never Reverse!
This is only true if you sincerely believe you have been given a
gift that is worthy to be shared with this world. If you just think
it would be cool or fun to be an actor or writer, good luck with
making it with that as the source of your power.

I hope after reading this chapter, you understand your
power source, keep your power on the right line, recharge
yourself by reigniting your power line, and finally, never give up
on striving for victory in every area of your life that is important
to you, even during the times when you feel disconnected
from yourself, your power source, or your friends or family.
It's how you respond to the catastrophes in life that give you
the tenacity to succeed. It is ridiculously easy in Hollywood to
get sidetracked by all the glitz n' glam the city and the industry
have to offer. It's easy to sync up your power with another
line because everyone does it. But, if you do what everyone
does, you will likely end up where most talent ends up, which
is not making it in Hollywood. The percentage of actors that
make it to A-list status is less than 1%, and according to SAG,
approximately 85% of actors are unemployed. The other 14%
are probably working actors but not quite at the A-list big bucks
status. Similar statistics also apply to the WGA, DGA and PGA,
which are the guilds for writers, directors and producers. Indeed,
these statistics should not undermine your desire to achieve
success in a cut-throat industry, but they should help you to
conceptualize the difficulty of making it in Hollywood.

Breaking into Hollywood is not the hard part; it's
staying there. They say it takes five to fifteen years to achieve
success. During that time, you must consistently refuel yourself
and your career; otherwise, the journey extends longer. I moved
to Hollywood almost nine years ago, and as I have said before,
I would not trade in my journey thus far for anything. But, I
surely plan to make my tenth year count. I hope you will join me
by making whatever year this is for you really count. We've got
the power!

eiGHTeeN

No Gas for the Next 100 Miles

When I reflect over the road trip from Chicago to Los Angeles that began my journey of breaking into Hollywood, I am always reminded of the gas sign I didn't believe: "No Gas for the Next 100 Miles." Every time I tell that story, people often ask why I didn't believe the sign. Even if I didn't believe it, one might question whether it would have been better for me to stop and get gas just in case there were no more gas stations ahead. From a safety standpoint, maybe that was the sensible thing to do. But my nicknames are Legally Blonde, Clueless and Lucy. If given the chance to relive the road trip, I would ignore the sign again. Call me crazy or even by my given nicknames if it makes you feel better. Without missing that sign, my E! True Hollywood story would not be as juicy.

I firmly believe our difficulties prepare us for our victories. The roommate from prison, weed head identity thief, sleepless nights, being out of a job multiple times with little cash on hand—all of these situations at the time seemed like horrendous struggles that I would not get through. But, I overcame them—all!

I encourage you to keep a journal of your experiences. What better way to inspire yourself than learning from your own journey. A book, movie, song, celebrity, mentor, family member or friend may be able to occasionally motivate you to pursue your dreams. But in order to sustain yourself in your pursuits, you must identify ways that will help you tackle challenges as they arise. You must find ways to continuously refuel your career.

While working as a talent agent, I can't tell you how often I came across actors with unrealistic plans. When I first joined the agency, I had the opportunity to interview over 100 actors. Initially, I only found about seven who caught my attention enough to sign them to my client roster. The actors I chose not to sign, most of them had unrealistic goals. Often, actors interviewing for possible representation would say they were going to make me so much money. The only way an actor could have made me a significant amount of money is if they booked about 10 national commercials a year, which is unrealistic for an actor at most levels.

The actors who I signed were those who had a plan of action for their career; those who knew whether they wanted to have a film career versus a theater career; those who set realistic goals that were within their control to achieve. It is an absolute must to establish realistic goals that are not only achievable, but also within your control. For example, to say you are going to book a national commercial in six months or land a co-star role in one year, although achievable, those are not goals in your control. However, submitting yourself for a certain amount of projects or increasing your network by meeting a certain number of industry professionals—those goals are achievable.

As a writer, having a goal of securing an agent this year is very much achievable; but it's not within your control. You must identify goals you can control such as sending out 50 query letters to agents, managers or producers. If you do this, you'll be far more progressive. Focus on being progressive and achieving daily successes.

There is no formula or recipe for breaking into Hollywood, but I would like to encourage you to embrace the entire journey.

As one minister said it best, "Learn to enjoy the entire road trip, even the bumps along the way."

When we ponder our dreams, we always think about the positive, never the negative. I don't believe you should have a Plan B in life. However, your Plan A should be detailed beyond belief and extremely realistic with mapped out solutions to possible road blocks that may present themselves along the journey of making your dreams come true.

Remember, Hollywood isn't going anywhere. The

only thing that leaves Hollywood are artistic professionals who originally came to L.A. with a dream and left feeling burnt out. Take your time breaking into Hollywood. Don't ignore the gas signs in your life. Fill up your tank with the highest level of octane by equipping yourself with the necessary tools needed to achieve success in your career and your personal life. None of us are perfect, but have you ever known anyone to achieve greatness by striving for imperfection? Today, make a commitment to go after your dream until you wake up the next morning and it feels surreal, but it's actually your life.

I'd like to share with you a conversation between my husband and I that ironically occurred while I was finishing the last chapter of this book.

"So, they didn't prosecute you?" Arthur asked with a straight face.

"Huh? Excuse me?" I replied.

He glanced at my laptop, acknowledging he was aware I was working on my book.

He repeated himself, "They didn't prosecute you yet—for breaking in?"

I giggled. "Have I officially broken in though? Maybe they haven't prosecuted me because I haven't broken in?"

"Of course you have," he said with confidence. "You weren't invited to Hollywood. You broke in the minute you packed your bags, drove cross-country by yourself, and arrived here."

My cherished reader, I hope you are more inspired to achieve your dream, especially if it appears difficult or impossible. No matter what obstacles or challenges you are facing, go after your dream until you achieve it. And even then, why not dream again and continue to excel.

As a thank you for traveling along my journey, I'd like to share with you the 'it' factor to breaking into Hollywood—dream it, pursue it, never quit it, and you will live it!

If you need any advice along your dream journey,
e-mail me at amh@breakingintohollywood.org.

aPPeNDiX

Highly recommended websites to explore.

Entertainment Organizations
www.breakingintohollywood.org *
www.changingimagesinamerica.org *
www.capeusa.org (Coalition of Asian Pacifics in Entertainment)
www.cinewomen.org
www.findfilm.org (Film Independent, formerly IFP)
www.hollywoodconnect.com *
www.nalip.org (National Association of Latino
Independent Producers)
www.obswriter.com (Organization of Black Screenwriters)
www.ScriptwritersNetwork.org *
www.wif.org (Women in Film)

Employment Websites
www.careerbuilders.com *
www.ComarAgency.com * (temp)
www.craigslist.org *
www.entertainmentcareers.net *
www.FriedmanPersonnel.com (temp)
www.journalismjobs.com *
www.mandy.com (casting notices too)
www.mediabistro.com
www.realitystaff.com
www.showbizjobs.com *
www.workplacehollywood.org * (perm)

Actor/Model/Talent Resources
www.ActorsAccess.com *
www.ActorsTips.com *
www.backstage.com
www.hollywoodnorth.com
www.LACasting.com *
www.NowCasting.com
www.sagindie.org *

Writing Fellowships/Mentorship Programs/ Filmmaker Labs*
www.abctalentdevelopment.com
www.cosbyprogram.com
www.emtags.com/site/www.cbsdiversity.com
www.findfilm.com
www.fox.com/diversity
www.nick.com/all_nick/fellowshipprogram
www.sundance.org
www.warnerbros.com/writersworkshop

Writer/Producer/Director Resources
www.826valencia.org
www.boxofficemojo.com *
www.centrotvandradio.com *
www.creativescreenwriting.com *
www.sagindie.org *
www.ScreenwritersUtopia.com
www.ScriptSales.com *
www.TriggerStreet.com *

Industry Resources
www.entertainmentpower.com
www.hcdonline.com *
www.imdb.com *
www.la411.com
www.media-services.com *
www.samuelfrench.com
www.thewritersstore.com *

Musician Resources
www.brooklynboy.com *
www.grammys.com *
www.lawim.com
www.NABFEME.org
www.narip.com